PIZZA NIGHT!

PIZZA NIGHT!

101 INCREDIBLE PIES TO MAKE AT HOME FROM THIN-CRUST TO DEEP-DISH
PLUS SAUCES, DOUGHS & SIDES

Oxmoor House®

WELCOME

Make tonight *Pizza Night!*

Everyone loves pizza! But not everyone loves takeout. The convenience is great but the flavor is often no better than the cardboard box it arrives in. Making your own pizza at home is easier—and there's no comparison where flavor's concerned. The best part? Making pizza with friends and family is FUN!

Whether you favor a simple, thin-crust margherita or a deep-dish supreme, this book delivers. The Pizzeria Classics chapter covers traditional favorites, Pizza Pronto offers super-fast preparations, and Pizzas with Pizzazz introduces unexpected flavor combos for the adventurous eater! We include directions for making pizza with a store-bought crust or from fresh homemade dough. Plus, any of these pizzas can be made gluten-free simply by starting with our recipe for Gluten-free Pizza Dough on page 17.

Once you've decided on your perfect pie, check out the "Little Helpers" boxes. These tips offer clever ways for kids to join the pizza-making party, making *Pizza Night!* a fun experience for the whole family. Add a scrumptious side from the delicious variety included throughout the book, then sit back and enjoy the compliments—and the pizza!

CONTENTS

WELCOME...**4**

PIZZA PRIMER...**6**
Make your pizza extra special with great homemade crusts
and easy sauces.

PIZZA PRONTO...**22**
Have dinner ready in 30 minutes or less with these
quick-and-simple pizzas.

PIZZERIA CLASSICS...**68**
These familiar favorites taste like you've just ordered them off
the menu of your local pizzeria.

PIZZAS WITH PIZZAZZ..................................**120**
Prepare to be "wowed" with the delicious and surprising
flavor combinations in these pizzas.

KIDS' FAVORITES...**178**
These simple, and sometimes silly, pizzas are sure to get the
whole family excited for dinner.

METRIC EQUIVALENTS...............................**218**

INDEX...**219**

PIZZA PRIMER

Make your pizza **extra special** with great homemade crusts and easy sauces.

BASIC TOMATO SAUCE

makes: 2⅔ cups   hands-on time: 30 min.   total time: 30 min.

Here's a super-easy sauce for pizzas and pastas. If you're making a pizza with lots of fun ingredients, this simple sauce won't compete with the other flavors.

4	to 5 garlic cloves, minced	1	(28-oz.) can crushed tomatoes
½	tsp. dried crushed red pepper	½	tsp. salt
2	Tbsp. extra virgin olive oil		

1. Sauté garlic and crushed pepper in hot oil in a large saucepan over medium heat 1 minute. (Do not brown garlic.) Stir in tomatoes and salt. Bring sauce to a boil, reduce heat to low, and simmer, stirring occasionally, 15 minutes.

Pizza Pointer

You can make this sauce up to a week ahead. Just let cool to room temperature, cover, and chill until you're ready to make a pizza!

BASIC PIZZA SAUCE

makes: 1⅓ cups   hands-on time: 10 min.   total time: 30 min.

A little white wine, some herbs, and a touch of balsamic vinegar give this sauce a deep, rich flavor. The sauce is perfect for a simple pizza so the flavor of the sauce can shine!

Vegetable cooking spray

¼   cup finely chopped onion

1   garlic clove, minced

¼   cup white wine

1   (14½-oz.) can undrained crushed tomatoes

2   Tbsp. tomato paste

1   tsp. dried oregano

⅛   tsp. freshly ground pepper

1   Tbsp. chopped fresh basil

½   tsp. balsamic vinegar

1. Heat a large saucepan over medium-high heat. Coat pan with cooking spray. Add onion to pan; sauté 3 minutes or until tender. Add minced garlic to pan; sauté 30 seconds. Stir in wine; cook 30 seconds.

2. Add crushed tomatoes and next 3 ingredients.

3. Reduce heat, and simmer 20 minutes or until thickened. Remove from heat; stir in basil and balsamic vinegar. Cool.

SPICY TOMATO PIZZA SAUCE

makes: 2 cups hands-on time: 5 min. total time: 30 min.

A real time-saver, this recipe makes enough sauce for two pizzas. Store any remaining sauce in an airtight container in refrigerator up to one week.

1   (28-oz.) can whole tomatoes

2   garlic cloves, minced

2   Tbsp. olive oil

1   Tbsp. chopped fresh basil

1   Tbsp. chopped fresh oregano

½   tsp. dried crushed red pepper

½   tsp. kosher salt

¼   tsp. freshly ground pepper

1. Crush tomatoes with a fork or with your hands, reserving juices.

2. Sauté garlic in hot oil in a medium saucepan 1 minute over medium heat. Add tomatoes with juice, basil, and next 4 ingredients; bring to a boil. Reduce heat, and simmer 20 to 25 minutes, stirring frequently, until sauce is reduced to 2 cups.

EASY ALFREDO SAUCE

makes: 1 cup   hands-on time: 8 min.   total time: 8 min.

This quick-start Alfredo sauce begins in a jar, but once you cook it up with garlic, basil, and freshly ground pepper, it will taste like you started from scratch.

1   garlic clove, minced

1   tsp. olive oil

1   (10-oz.) container refrigerated Alfredo sauce

1   Tbsp. chopped fresh or 1 tsp. dried basil

½   tsp. freshly ground pepper

1. Sauté garlic in hot oil in a large skillet over medium-high heat 1 minute. Reduce heat to medium-low; stir in remaining ingredients. Cook, stirring constantly, 2 minutes or until thoroughly heated.

Note: We tested with Buitoni Alfredo Sauce.

PIZZA POINTER

This sauce can be made ahead, covered and chilled, up to 5 days. Reheat in a saucepan over medium-low heat.

BASIL PESTO

makes: 2 cups hands-on time: 10 min. total time: 10 min.

Use this pesto recipe on a pizza instead of pizza sauce. You can also use it to stir some summertime goodness into hot cooked pasta, rice, or grits, or even spread it on garlic bread.

2 cups loosely packed fresh basil leaves

1 cup grated Parmesan cheese

⅔ cup olive oil

¼ cup pine nuts

2 garlic cloves

3 Tbsp. cold water

1 Tbsp. lemon juice

½ tsp. salt

1. Process all ingredients in a food processor until smooth, stopping to scrape down sides as necessary.

PIZZA POINTER

This may sound like a lot of basil, but you need all of it. Use bright green, fresh basil leaves, and you'll be rewarded with flavor-packed pesto that's delicious on just about anything.

AWESOME FLAVOR!

SUN-DRIED TOMATO PESTO

makes: 1½ cups   hands-on time: 10 min.   total time: 10 min.

This zesty pesto is a flavorful substitute for pizza sauce. The sun-dried tomatoes have a rich, sweet flavor that's perfect on a veggie or cheesy pizza.

2   (3-oz.) packages sun-dried tomato halves

½   cup grated Parmesan cheese

½   cup loosely packed fresh flat-leaf parsley

½   cup olive oil

¼   cup pine nuts

3   garlic cloves

3   Tbsp. cold water

1   Tbsp. lemon juice

1. Process all ingredients in a food processor until smooth, stopping to scrape down sides as necessary.

PIZZA POINTER

You can make this sauce up to a week ahead. Cover and chill until ready to use.

EASY PIZZA DOUGH

makes: 6 (8-inch) pizza dough rounds hands-on time: 10 min. total time: 2 hours, 10 min.

You can make the dough up to 24 hours before you need it, or follow directions below to make it up to three months ahead.

1	**cup warm water (100° to 110°)**
¼	**cup olive oil**
1	**(¼-oz.) envelope active dry yeast**
2	**tsp. honey**
3½	**cups all-purpose flour**
1	**tsp. kosher salt**
	Vegetable cooking spray

Pizza Pointer

To make this pizza ahead, bake dough rounds at 400° for 7 minutes. Freeze crusts in zip-top plastic bags for up to three months.

1. Process first 4 ingredients in a food processor 20 seconds or until yeast is dissolved and mixture is bubbly. Add flour and salt; pulse 6 to 8 times or until dough forms a ball and pulls away from sides of bowl, adding more water if necessary.

2. Place dough in a large bowl coated with cooking spray; lightly coat dough with cooking spray. Cover and chill at least 2 hours or up to 24 hours.

3. Place dough on a lightly floured surface. Divide dough into 6 equal portions; roll each portion into an 8-inch round. Use dough immediately, or follow instructions at left to make ahead.

GLUTEN-FREE PIZZA DOUGH

makes: 1 (12-inch) pizza dough round hands-on time: 15 min. total time: 15 min.

Turn almost any pizza into a gluten-free pizza by substituting the crust for this simple dough.

- 1 (¼-oz.) envelope active dry yeast
- 2½ tsp. sugar, divided
- 1 cup warm soy milk or 2% reduced-fat milk (100° to 110°)
- 4.4 oz. brown rice flour (about 1 cup), divided
- ½ cup cornstarch
- 2 tsp. xanthan gum
- 1 tsp. dried Italian seasoning
- ½ tsp. fine sea salt
- 1 Tbsp. olive oil, divided
- 2 tsp. apple cider vinegar

1. Dissolve yeast and ½ tsp. sugar in warm milk in a small bowl; let stand 5 minutes.

2. Weigh 3.3 oz. brown rice flour (or lightly spoon ¾ cup brown rice flour into dry measuring cup; level with a knife). Place brown rice flour, remaining 2 tsp. sugar, cornstarch, and next 3 ingredients in a food processor. With processor on, pour yeast mixture, olive oil, and vinegar through food chute; process 30 seconds, adding brown rice flour, 1 Tbsp. at a time if necessary, until mixture forms a ball. Use immediately.

WHOLE WHEAT PIZZA DOUGH

makes: 1 (12-inch) pizza dough round hands-on time: 12 min. total time: 1 hour, 22 min.

1¼ tsp. active dry yeast

⅔ cup warm water (100°
    to 110°)

1 cup all-purpose flour

¾ cup whole wheat flour

1½ tsp. sea salt

1 tsp. honey

2 to 3 tsp. extra virgin
    olive oil

To make this dough ahead, prepare recipe as directed through Step 2. After allowing the dough to rise, punch it down and refrigerate it overnight. Allow the dough to come to room temperature before using.

1. Combine yeast and warm water in bowl of a heavy-duty electric stand mixer. Let stand 5 minutes or until foamy. Add flours and salt to yeast mixture; beat at low speed (using a dough hook attachment) until smooth and blended. Add honey and 2 tsp. olive oil; beat at low speed 2 minutes. Gradually add remaining 1 tsp. olive oil, if needed, to make a soft dough. Beat at medium speed 4 minutes or until dough forms a ball and pulls away from sides of bowl. Knead dough on a well-floured surface until smooth and elastic (about 5 minutes). (Dough should be slightly sticky.)

2. Place dough in a well-greased bowl, turning to grease top. Cover dough with plastic wrap, and let rise in a warm place (85°), free from drafts, 1 hour or until doubled in bulk.

3. Punch dough down; let stand 5 minutes. Shape into a ball.

BRICK OVEN PIZZA DOUGH

makes: 2 (14-inch) pizza crusts hands-on time: 40 min. total time: 2 hours

This pizza dough is best baked in a pizza oven but can also be made in a conventional oven with great success!

- 2 (¼-oz.) envelopes active dry yeast
- 2 cups warm water (100° to 110°)
- 5 cups all-purpose unbleached flour, divided
- 1 cup coarse-ground whole wheat flour
- 2 tsp. salt
- 2 tsp. sugar
- 1½ tsp. dried thyme
- ⅓ cup grated Parmesan cheese (optional)
- ½ cup plus 3 Tbsp. extra virgin olive oil, divided

1. Combine yeast and warm water in a 2-cup liquid measuring cup, and let stand 5 minutes.

2. Combine yeast mixture, 3 cups all-purpose flour, whole-wheat flour, next 3 ingredients, and, if desired, cheese in a large mixing bowl; add ½ cup olive oil. Beat at low speed with an electric mixer until blended, stopping to scrape down sides as necessary. Stir in enough remaining all-purpose flour (about ⅓ cup) to make a stiff dough. (Dough will be smooth.)

3. Place dough and 1 Tbsp. oil in a large, lightly greased bowl, turning to coat top. Cover and let rise in a warm place (85°), free from drafts, 45 minutes or until dough is doubled in bulk. Punch dough down.

4. Preheat oven to 500°. Turn dough out onto a lightly floured surface, and knead 4 or 5 times. Divide dough in half, and shape into balls. Roll each ball into a 14-inch circle on a lightly floured surface. Place one 14-inch circle onto a lightly floured pizza peel; brush with 1 Tbsp. oil, and prick with a fork. Punch dough down, and shape according to directions in desired recipe.

5. Place pizza gently on floor of brick oven. Repeat procedure with remaining dough circle, and place on floor of brick oven.

6. Bake each pizza at 500° for 5 to 7 minutes or until browned and bubbly.

Pizza Pointer

To bake in a conventional oven, place dough on a lightly floured pizza stone or baking sheet, and bake at 475° for 10 to 12 minutes.

SOURDOUGH PIZZA DOUGH

makes: 1 (12-inch) pizza dough round
hands-on time: 6 min. total time: 1 hour, plus 1 day for starter and primary batter

If you are serious about homemade pizza from start to finish, this is the crust for you. The addition of sourdough gives this crust an artisan flavor.

1½ **cups Sourdough Primary Batter**

1½ **cups all-purpose flour**

1½ **tsp. kosher salt**

2 **Tbsp. extra virgin olive oil**

PIZZA POINTER

To make dough ahead, divide risen dough in half before kneading, and wrap in plastic wrap. Place in zip-top freezer bags; freeze up to 3 months. Thaw overnight in refrigerator.

1. Combine all ingredients in bowl of a heavy-duty electric stand mixer. Beat at low speed until smooth and blended. Beat at medium speed 1 minute.

2. Turn dough out onto a well-floured surface, and knead until smooth and elastic (about 4 to 6 minutes, sprinkling surface with flour as needed).

3. Place dough in a greased bowl, turning to grease top. Cover with plastic wrap; let rise in a warm place (85°), free from drafts, 1 to 1½ hours or until doubled in bulk and dough is springy when lightly touched. Punch dough down, and shape according to directions in desired recipe.

Sourdough Primary Batter

makes: 2 cups hands-on time: 10 min. total time: 8 hours, 10 min.

1 **cup Sourdough Starter**	1½ **cups all-purpose flour**
1 **cup warm water (85°)**	

1. Place 1 cup Sourdough Starter in a large, warm bowl. Cover remaining starter, and return to refrigerator. Stir warm water (85°) into starter in bowl. Add flour, ½ cup at a time, stirring well after each addition. Cover and place in a warm place (85°), free from drafts, 8 to 10 hours. Batter should have many large bubbles and have a yeasty, slightly sour yet pleasant odor, when it is ready to use. Measure out 1½ cups Sourdough Primary Batter for Sourdough Pizza Dough, returning remaining batter (at least 1 cup) to Sourdough Starter in refrigerator. Store covered in coldest part of refrigerator. (This feeds the starter to keep it going.)

Note: Repeat this procedure for use in future recipes. (Always remember to return at least 1 cup batter to starter before preparing a recipe.) Sourdough Starter can be maintained in this manner indefinitely. Always remove starter from storage container and wash container well with each use. Return starter to clean container.

Sourdough Starter

makes: about 2 cups hands-on time: 10 min. total time: 10 hours, 15 min.

1 **(¼-oz.) envelope active dry yeast**	2 **cups warm water (100° to 110°)**
1 **Tbsp. sugar**	2 **cups all-purpose flour**

1. Dissolve yeast and sugar in 1 cup warm water in a medium-size glass bowl, stirring well. Let stand 5 minutes or until bubbly. Gradually add remaining 1 cup warm water and flour; mix well using a wooden spoon. Cover with plastic wrap, and let stand in a warm place (85°), free from drafts, 10 to 12 hours. Label fermented mixture, and store in refrigerator. Stir daily; use within 10 days to prepare Sourdough Primary Batter.

PIZZA PRONTO

Have dinner ready in
30 minutes or less
with these quick-and-simple pizzas.

MUSHROOM PIZZA STICKS

makes: 2 servings (6 sticks per serving) hands-on time: 7 min. total time: 17 min.

This healthier version of pizza sticks is perfect for an after-school snack for the kids or a casual family gathering.

1   (8.8-oz.) package whole-wheat naan flatbreads, each cut into 1¼-inch strips

Cooking spray

½   cup pizza sauce

½   (8-oz.) package cremini mushrooms, chopped

1   cup (4 oz.) shredded part-skim mozzarella cheese

Oregano leaves (optional)

Additional pizza sauce (optional)

1. Preheat oven to 450°.

2. Place naan strips on a baking sheet coated with cooking spray. Spread sauce evenly over strips; sprinkle with mushrooms, and top with cheese.

3. Bake at 450° for 10 minutes or until golden brown and bubbly. Garnish with oregano, and serve with additional pizza sauce, if desired.

Look for packaged naan in the deli section of your local market. It's a new twist on pizza crust that saves time and tastes great!

SPEED IT UP!

MINI WHITE PIZZAS
WITH VEGETABLES

makes: 4 servings   hands-on time: 5 min.   total time: 14 min.

Whole wheat pita rounds help speed up this recipe and add a nutty flavor.

4   (6-inch) whole wheat pitas

Olive oil-flavored cooking spray

1   medium zucchini, thinly sliced

¼   cup thinly sliced red onion, separated into rings

¼   tsp. freshly ground pepper

⅛   tsp. salt

½   cup buttery garlic-and-herbs spreadable cheese

6   Tbsp. shredded Asiago cheese

1. Preheat broiler. Place pitas on a baking sheet; broil 1 to 2 minutes or until lightly toasted (check often so as not to burn).

2. Heat a nonstick skillet over medium-high heat; coat pan with cooking spray. Add zucchini, onion, pepper, and salt; sauté 3 minutes or until vegetables are crisp-tender.

3. Remove pitas from oven, and spread 2 Tbsp. garlic-and-herbs spreadable cheese over each pita. Top evenly with vegetables and Asiago cheese. Broil 1 to 2 minutes or until edges are lightly browned and cheese melts.

Note: We tested with Alouette Garlic & Herbs spreadable cheese.

PIZZA POINTER

For a Greek-inspired flavor variation, substitute hummus for the spreadable cheese.

ROASTED VEGETABLE PIZZA

makes: 6 servings   hands-on time: 5 min.   total time: 35 min.

Roast the grape tomatoes and zucchini ahead, and refrigerate. Use the mixture as a topping for this hearty pizza or as a side dish for grilled chicken or fish.

3   cups Roasted Zucchini & Tomatoes

1   (10-oz.) Italian cheese-flavored thin pizza crust

⅓   cup jarred pesto sauce

1   cup (4 oz.) pre-shredded part-skim mozzarella cheese

2   Tbsp. grated fresh Parmesan cheese

1. Preheat oven to 500°. Prepare Roasted Zucchini and Tomatoes. Place pizza crust on rack in oven while preheating, and heat 5 minutes.

2. Remove crust from oven; place on an ungreased baking sheet. Spread pesto evenly over crust. Top with Roasted Zucchini and Tomatoes; sprinkle evenly with cheeses.

3. Bake at 500° for 7 minutes or until cheeses melt.

ROASTED ZUCCHINI & TOMATOES

makes: 3 cups
hands-on time: 4 min.
total time: 22 min.

1   (8-oz.) container refrigerated prechopped red onion

2   medium zucchini, coarsely chopped

1   cup grape tomatoes

2   tsp. olive oil

¼   tsp. salt

¼   tsp. pepper

1   Tbsp. chopped fresh basil

1. Preheat oven to 500°. Combine first 6 ingredients; toss well. Spread vegetable mixture on a large rimmed baking sheet.

2. Bake at 500° for 18 minutes or until vegetables are tender and lightly browned, stirring after 12 minutes. Add basil to roasted vegetables; toss gently.

PITA PIZZAS
WITH SPINACH, FONTINA & ONIONS

makes: 4 servings hands-on time: 9 min. total time: 15 min.

Fontina, a creamy Italian cheese, has a nutty flavor and silky texture. It's a perfect topping for pizza because it melts so easily.

3 tsp. olive oil, divided

3 garlic cloves, minced

2 cups vertically sliced red onion

2 cups baby spinach leaves

4 (7-inch) whole wheat pitas

¼ cup (1 oz.) shredded fontina cheese

1. Preheat oven to 450°.

2. Heat 1 tsp. olive oil in a medium nonstick skillet over medium-high heat. Add garlic and onion; sauté 5 minutes or until tender.

3. Add spinach, and sauté 2 minutes or just until spinach begins to wilt. Remove from heat.

4. Place pitas on a large baking sheet; brush with remaining 2 tsp. olive oil. Top pitas evenly with garlic-spinach mixture and cheese. Bake at 450° for 4 minutes or until cheese melts and pitas are browned.

serve with
GREEK PASTA SALAD

makes: 6 to 8 servings
hands-on time: 10 min.
total time: 15 min.

1 (12-oz.) package angel hair pasta

1 (6-oz.) package feta cheese, crumbled

1 (4-oz.) jar diced pimientos, drained

1 (2½-oz.) can sliced black olives, drained

6 green onions, thinly sliced

½ cup Italian dressing

1. Prepare pasta according to package directions. Toss pasta with remaining ingredients. Serve immediately, or cover and chill up to 2 days.

ONLY 5-MINUTE PREP TIME!

ROASTED MUSHROOM & SHALLOT PIZZA

makes: 6 servings hands-on time: 5 min. total time: 35 min.

2 cups Roasted Mushrooms & Shallots

½ (8-oz.) container light chive-and-onion cream cheese

1 (10-oz.) cheese-flavored thin pizza crust

3 (1-oz.) slices reduced-fat Lorraine cheese

2 Tbsp. fresh oregano leaves

1. Preheat oven to 450°. Prepare Roasted Mushrooms & Shallots.

2. Spread cream cheese over pizza crust. Top with Roasted Mushrooms & Shallots and cheese slices.

3. Bake pizza at 450° directly on oven rack 8 minutes or until crust is golden and cheese melts. Sprinkle with oregano, and serve immediately.

PIZZA POINTER

Lorraine cheese, which comes in long slices, is similar in flavor to Swiss cheese.

ROASTED MUSHROOMS & SHALLOTS

makes: 2 cups
hands-on time: 8 min.
total time: 23 min.

1 (8-oz.) package baby portobello mushrooms, quartered

1 (3.5-oz.) package shiitake mushrooms, stems removed and quartered

2 (3-oz.) packages small shallots, peeled and quartered lengthwise

1 Tbsp. extra virgin olive oil

¾ tsp. freshly ground black pepper

¼ tsp. salt

4 garlic cloves, minced

1. Preheat oven to 450°. Combine all ingredients in a large bowl.

2. Spread mushroom mixture in a single layer on a lightly greased jelly-roll pan.

3. Bake at 450° for 15 minutes. Do not stir.

GARLIC-MASHED POTATO PIZZA

makes: 4 servings hands-on time: 4 min. total time: 30 min.

Tomato Topping

1½ cups country-style refrigerated mashed potatoes

1 Tbsp. bottled roasted minced garlic

¼ tsp. freshly ground black pepper

1 (10-oz.) thin pizza crust

Olive oil–flavored cooking spray

1. Preheat oven to 450°. Prepare Tomato Topping.

2. Place potatoes in a microwave-safe bowl. Cover with plastic wrap; vent. Microwave at HIGH 3 minutes or until thoroughly heated, stirring after 1½ minutes. Stir in garlic and pepper.

3. While potatoes cook, coat crust with cooking spray. Spread potato mixture onto crust to within 1 inch of edge. Sprinkle Tomato Topping over pizza.

4. Bake pizza at 450°, directly on oven rack, for 8 minutes or until crust is browned.

Note: We tested with Simply Potatoes.

TOMATO TOPPING

makes: 4 servings
hands-on time: 1 min.
total time: 16 min.

2 cups grape tomatoes

2 tsp. olive oil

¼ tsp. salt

¼ tsp. freshly ground black pepper

¼ tsp. crushed red pepper

1 Tbsp. chopped fresh rosemary

1. Preheat oven to 450°. Spread tomatoes on a rimmed baking sheet; drizzle with oil. Sprinkle with salt and peppers; toss gently.

2. Bake at 450° for 15 minutes (do not stir). Sprinkle with rosemary.

FUN FLAVOR COMBO!

BALSAMIC VEGETABLE PITA PIZZAS

makes: 4 servings hands-on time: 6 min. total time: 15 min.

A new take on pizza, this recipe uses pita bread and hummus topped with sautéed vegetables and goat cheese.

- 4 (6-inch) whole wheat pitas
- Balsamic Vegetables
- ½ cup hummus
- ½ cup (2 oz.) crumbled goat cheese

1. Preheat oven to 450°.

2. Arrange pitas on a large baking sheet. Bake at 450° for 2 to 3 minutes or until pitas are toasted.

3. Prepare Balsamic Vegetables.

4. Spread 2 Tbsp. hummus over each pita. Top evenly with Balsamic Vegetables and goat cheese. Serve immediately.

BALSAMIC VEGETABLES

makes: 4 servings
hands-on time: 10 min.
total time: 10 min.

- 1 Tbsp. olive oil
- 1 medium zucchini, halved lengthwise and sliced
- 1 medium-size yellow squash, halved lengthwise and sliced
- 1 cup sliced fresh cremini mushrooms
- ½ cup red bell pepper strips
- ½ cup sliced red onion
- 2 Tbsp. balsamic vinegar
- ¼ tsp. salt
- ¼ tsp. freshly ground pepper

1. Heat oil in a large nonstick skillet over medium-high heat. Add zucchini and next 4 ingredients. Sauté 5 minutes or until vegetables are tender. Stir in vinegar, salt, and pepper; sauté 1 more minute.

GARDEN EGGPLANT PIZZA

makes: 6 servings   hands-on time: 20 min.   total time: 30 min.

1   large eggplant, peeled and coarsely chopped

1   medium tomato, coarsely chopped

1   red bell pepper, coarsely chopped

1   onion, chopped

1   small zucchini, coarsely chopped

3   Tbsp. olive oil, divided

1   (14-oz.) Italian pizza crust

2   cups (8 oz.) shredded mozzarella cheese

½   tsp. dried basil

½   tsp. dried oregano

½   tsp. dried thyme

½   tsp. salt

¼   tsp. garlic powder

¼   tsp. freshly ground pepper

1. Preheat oven to 425°. Sauté eggplant and next 4 ingredients in 1 Tbsp. oil in a large skillet over medium-high heat 10 minutes or until tender.

2. Layer pizza crust evenly with cheese and eggplant mixture; sprinkle with basil and next 5 ingredients. Drizzle with remaining 2 Tbsp. oil.

3. Bake at 425° for 10 minutes or crust is until golden brown.

Get a jump start on this pizza by buying prechopped tomatoes, red peppers, and onion from the produce section of your local grocery.

SPEED IT UP!

GOAT CHEESE, TOMATO & BASIL PIZZA

makes: 6 servings   hands-on time: 5 min.   total time: 15 min.

This pizza gets its fresh, flavorful taste from marinara sauce, creamy goat cheese, and juicy grape tomatoes. Vary the flavor by substituting your favorite pasta sauce.

1   (10-oz.) Italian cheese-flavored thin pizza crust

Vegetable cooking spray

¾   cup marinara sauce

1¼   cups (5 oz.) crumbled goat cheese

¾   cup grape tomatoes, halved lengthwise

2   Tbsp. small basil leaves

Freshly ground pepper

1. Preheat oven to 450°. Place pizza crust on an ungreased baking sheet; lightly coat crust with cooking spray. Spread sauce evenly over crust.

2. Sprinkle cheese and tomatoes over crust. Slide pizza off pan directly onto oven rack.

3. Bake at 450° for 10 minutes or until crust is golden and crisp. Carefully slide pizza from oven rack back onto pan using a spatula. Sprinkle pizza with basil and pepper.

Let kids help spread sauce over dough, sprinkle with cheese, and place tomatoes on top of pizza.

LITTLE HELPERS

TOMATO, ASPARAGUS & BASIL PIZZA

makes: 4 servings hands-on time: 10 min. total time: 25 min.

½   lb. asparagus, cut into 1½-inch pieces (about 1 cup)

1   (10-oz.) Italian cheese-flavored thin pizza crust

Vegetable cooking spray

2   Tbsp. jarred pesto sauce

6   plum tomatoes, cut into ¼-inch-thick slices (about ¾ lb.)

1   cup (4 oz.) shredded part-skim mozzarella cheese

¼   cup thinly sliced fresh basil

1. Preheat oven to 450°. Steam asparagus, covered, 2 minutes or until crisp-tender. Rinse under cold running water; drain well, and pat dry with paper towels.

2. Place pizza crust on an ungreased pizza pan or baking sheet. Lightly coat pizza crust with cooking spray. Spread pesto evenly over crust. Arrange tomato slices and asparagus pieces over pesto. Sprinkle with cheese. Bake at 450° for 15 minutes or until cheese melts and pizza is thoroughly heated. Remove from oven, and sprinkle with basil.

PIZZA POINTER

If you want to get a jump start on this recipe, steam asparagus, and keep covered and chilled up to 1 day ahead. When you're ready to make the pizza, just add toppings and bake.

serve with
MIXED GREENS WITH DIJON VINAIGRETTE

makes: 4 cups
hands-on time: 5 min.
total time: 5 min.

1   Tbsp. balsamic vinegar

1   Tbsp. olive oil

1   tsp. honey

⅓   tsp. Dijon mustard

⅛   tsp. coarsely ground pepper

4   cups mixed salad greens

½   cup seedless red grape halves

1. Whisk together first 5 ingredients in a large bowl until blended. Add mixed salad greens; toss gently. Divide greens mixture among 4 salad plates; top with red seedless grape halves.

GRILLED HEIRLOOM TOMATO PIZZA

makes: 6 servings   hands-on time: 11 min.   total time: 15 min.

Compared to their grocery-store counterparts, heirloom tomatoes are both flavorful and colorful—you'll find them in red, orange, gold, taxi yellow, nearly white, pink, purplish black, and green. Your choice of tomato will shine in this simple pizza.

1   (13.8-oz.) can refrigerated pizza crust dough

Vegetable cooking spray

1   garlic clove, halved

1   large heirloom tomato, seeded and chopped (about 10 oz.)

½   cup (2 oz.) shredded part-skim mozzarella cheese

¾   cup (3 oz.) crumbled herbed goat cheese

1. Preheat grill to 300° to 350° (medium) heat.

2. Unroll dough onto a large baking sheet coated with cooking spray; pat dough into a 12- x 9-inch rectangle. Lightly coat dough with cooking spray.

3. Place dough on grill rack coated with cooking spray; grill 1 minute or until lightly browned. Turn crust over. Rub with garlic; sprinkle with tomato and cheeses. Grill, covered with grill lid, 3 minutes. Serve immediately.

Make this pizza even faster by buying prechopped tomatoes from the produce section of your local market.

SPEED It Up!

SUNNY-SIDE-UP PIZZA

makes: 6 servings hands-on time: 30 min. total time: 44 min.

Pizza for breakfast? This pie would certainly be a great one to try in the morning or for a brunch with a side salad.

1   lb. refrigerated fresh pizza dough, at room temperature

2   Tbsp. olive oil, divided

2   garlic cloves, minced

6   large eggs

⅛   tsp. kosher salt

4   cups mâche or baby spinach

¼   cup thinly sliced red onion

3   Tbsp. balsamic vinaigrette

½   cup (2 oz.) shaved fresh Parmesan cheese

⅜   tsp. pepper

1. Preheat oven to 450°.

2. Roll dough into a 14-inch circle on a lightly floured surface. Place on a pizza pan; pierce with a fork. Combine 1½ Tbsp. oil and garlic; brush over dough. Bake at 450° for 14 minutes.

3. Heat a large nonstick skillet over medium heat. Add remaining 1½ tsp. oil; swirl to coat. Gently break eggs into pan; cook 4 minutes or until whites are set. Sprinkle with salt.

4. Combine mâche, onion, and vinaigrette. Arrange on crust; top with eggs, cheese, and pepper. Serve immediately.

PIZZA POINTER

Cooking the eggs just until the whites are set means the yolks will provide a tasty, runny sauce when they're broken.

SHRIMP PIZZA

makes: 4 servings   hands-on time: 10 min.   total time: 30 min.

Pizza gets a taste of the sea with poached shrimp—sure to please seafood lovers and land lovers alike. Prepare shrimp ahead, and keep refrigerated until ready to use.

1   (14-oz.) Italian pizza crust

⅓   cup refrigerated light pesto sauce or Alfredo sauce

10 to 12 Perfect Poached Shrimp, peeled

½   cup coarsely chopped jarred roasted red bell peppers

⅓   cup freshly grated Parmesan cheese

1   cup loosely packed arugula

Shaved Parmesan cheese

Freshly ground pepper

1. Preheat oven to 450°. Spread pizza crust with pesto or Alfredo sauce. Top with Perfect Poached Shrimp, chopped roasted red bell peppers, and ⅓ cup freshly grated Parmesan cheese.

2. Bake at 450° for 20 minutes or until thoroughly heated. Top with arugula, shaved Parmesan cheese, and pepper.

PERFECT POACHED SHRIMP

makes: 3 to 4 servings
hands-on time: 15 min.
total time: 30 min.

Ice

1   lemon, halved

1   Tbsp. black peppercorns

2   bay leaves

2   tsp. salt

2   lb. unpeeled, large raw shrimp

1. Fill a large bowl halfway with ice and water. Pour 4 quarts water into a Dutch oven; squeeze juice from lemon into Dutch oven. Stir in lemon halves, black peppercorns, bay leaves, and salt; bring to a boil over medium-high heat. Remove from heat; add shrimp. Cover and let stand 5 minutes or just until shrimp turn pink. Stir shrimp into ice water; let stand 10 minutes. Peel and devein shrimp.

PEACH & GORGONZOLA CHICKEN PIZZA

makes: 4 servings hands-on time: 7 min. total time: 23 min.

Give pizza a makeover by topping with fresh peach slices and two types of cheese. A drizzle of tangy balsamic reduction perfectly balances the sweet summer fruit.

1   (10-oz.) thin pizza crust

Vegetable cooking spray

1   tsp. extra virgin olive oil

½   cup (2 oz.) shredded part-skim mozzarella cheese, divided

1   cup shredded cooked chicken breast

⅓   cup (about 1½ oz.) crumbled Gorgonzola cheese

1   medium unpeeled peach, thinly sliced

⅓   cup balsamic vinegar

1. Preheat oven to 400°. Place pizza crust on a baking sheet coated with cooking spray. Brush oil evenly over crust. Top evenly with ¼ cup mozzarella, chicken, Gorgonzola, and peach slices. Top with remaining ¼ cup mozzarella.

2. Bake at 400° for 11 minutes or until crust is golden.

3. Place vinegar in a small saucepan over medium-high heat; cook until reduced to 2 Tbsp. (about 5 minutes). Drizzle balsamic reduction evenly over pizza.

serve with

SPINACH SALAD WITH BALSAMIC DRESSING

makes: 6 cups
hands-on time: 5 min.
total time: 5 min.

2   Tbsp. minced shallots

1   Tbsp. olive oil

1   Tbsp. balsamic vinegar

⅛   tsp. salt

6   cups fresh baby spinach

1. Whisk together first 4 ingredients in a large bowl. Add baby spinach; toss well.

EASY PIZZA SQUARES

makes: 4 servings hands-on time: 10 min. total time: 35 min.

1 (13.8-oz.) can refrigerated pizza crust dough

1½ cups (6 oz.) shredded Mexican four-cheese blend, divided

⅔ cup mayonnaise

2 Tbsp. chopped fresh basil

2 tsp. jarred minced garlic

¼ tsp. dried Italian seasoning

⅛ tsp. salt

4 plum tomatoes, thinly sliced

1. Preheat oven to 350°. Press pizza crust out onto a lightly greased baking sheet.

2. Bake at 350° for 10 minutes or until lightly browned.

3. Increase oven temperature to 375°. Stir together 1 cup cheese, mayonnaise, and next 4 ingredients; spread mixture over pizza crust. Arrange tomato slices over crust, and sprinkle with remaining ½ cup cheese.

4. Bake at 375° for 15 minutes.

This is a great recipe that kids can make! Parents can help slice tomatoes and bake the pizza, but kids can do the rest.

Little Helpers

serve with

SPINACH-AND-RED-PEPPER SAUTÉ

makes: 2 cups
hands-on time: 10 min.
total time: 10 min.

1 Tbsp. olive oil

3 (10-oz.) packages fresh spinach

2 garlic cloves

½ (12-oz.) jar roasted red bell peppers, drained and chopped

¼ cup pine nuts, toasted

½ tsp. salt

¼ tsp. pepper

1. Heat oil in a nonstick skillet over medium heat.

2. Sauté spinach and garlic cloves, pressed, over medium-high heat 4 to 5 minutes or until spinach wilts. Drain well.

3. Stir in roasted red bell peppers, pine nuts, salt, and pepper.

CHICKEN FAJITA PIZZA

makes: 4 to 6 servings   hands-on time: 15 min.   total time: 27 min.

1   (14-oz.) Italian pizza crust

2   skinned and boned chicken breasts, cut into strips

1   Tbsp. vegetable oil

2   tsp. chili powder

1   tsp. salt

½   tsp. garlic powder

1   small onion, sliced

1   small green bell pepper, chopped

1   cup salsa

1   (8-oz.) package shredded Monterey Jack cheese

Toppings: chopped tomatoes, shredded lettuce, sour cream

1. Preheat oven to 425°. Place crust on a lightly greased baking sheet.

2. Sauté chicken in hot oil in a skillet over medium-high heat 5 minutes or until tender. Stir in chili powder, salt, and garlic powder. Remove from skillet, and set aside.

3. Add onion and bell pepper to skillet; sauté 5 minutes or until tender.

4. Spread crust with salsa; top with chicken, onion mixture, and cheese. Bake at 425° for 10 to 12 minutes or until cheese melts. Serve with desired toppings.

serve with

ARUGULA-GRAPE TOMATO SALAD

makes: 5 cups
hands-on time: 4 min.
total time: 4 min.

1   (5-oz.) package arugula

3   pt. grape tomatoes

2   Tbsp. fresh lemon juice

2   Tbsp. olive oil

½   tsp. salt

1. Toss together all ingredients. Serve immediately.

Get this pizza on the table even faster by using 2 Tbsp. taco seasoning instead of the chili powder, salt, and garlic powder.

SPEED IT UP!

BISTRO GRILLED CHICKEN PIZZA

makes: 6 servings hands-on time: 15 min. total time: 25 min.

The rectangular shape, grilled crust, and fun toppings like feta, fresh basil, and chicken make this pizza taste like something you would order at a restaurant!

1 **(13.8-oz.) can refrigerated pizza crust dough**

1 **tsp. olive oil**

¾ **cup pizza sauce**

4 **plum tomatoes, sliced**

2 **cups chopped rotisserie chicken**

1 **(4-oz.) package tomato-and-basil feta cheese**

1 **cup (4 oz.) shredded mozzarella cheese**

2 **Tbsp. small fresh basil leaves**

Pizza Pointer

Use long-handled grilling tongs and a spatula to turn the dough with ease.

1. Preheat grill to 300° to 350° (medium) heat. Unroll dough, and place on a lightly greased 18- x 12-inch sheet of heavy-duty aluminum foil. Starting at center, press out dough with hands to form a 13- x 9-inch rectangle. Brush dough evenly with olive oil.

2. Invert dough onto cooking grate; peel off foil. Grill, covered with grill lid, 2 to 3 minutes or until bottom of dough is golden brown. Turn dough over, and grill, covered with grill lid, 1 to 2 minutes or until bottom is set. Carefully remove crust from grill to an aluminum foil-lined baking sheet.

3. Microwave pizza sauce in a small glass bowl at HIGH 30 seconds or until warm, stirring once. Spread sauce evenly over crust; top with tomato slices and chicken. Sprinkle evenly with cheeses. Return pizza to cooking grate (pizza should slide easily). Grill, covered with grill lid, 3 to 5 more minutes or until crust is done and cheese is melted. Sprinkle with basil leaves.

BARBECUE CHICKEN PIZZA

makes: 6 servings   hands-on time: 24 min.   total time: 44 min.

1   small onion, chopped

½   red bell pepper, chopped

½   tsp. salt

¼   tsp. pepper

1   tsp. olive oil

1   (13.8-oz.) can refrigerated pizza crust dough

½   cup hickory smoke barbecue sauce

2   (6-oz.) packages grilled boneless, skinless chicken breast strips

2   cups (8 oz.) shredded pepper Jack cheese

Garnish: chopped fresh parsley

Hickory smoke barbecue sauce

1. Preheat oven to 400°. Sauté first 4 ingredients in hot oil in a large skillet over medium-high heat 8 to 10 minutes or until vegetables are tender. Drain well.

2. Unroll pizza crust; press or pat into a lightly greased 13- x 9-inch pan.

3. Bake crust at 400° for 12 to 14 minutes. Spread ½ cup barbecue sauce evenly over top of pizza crust in pan. Arrange chicken strips evenly over barbecue sauce, top with onion mixture, and sprinkle evenly with cheese.

4. Bake at 400° for 8 to 10 minutes or until cheese melts. Garnish, if desired. Serve with extra sauce for dipping.

By using precooked and sliced chicken, like Tyson Grilled & Ready chicken breast strips, you'll save valuable time and effort.

Speed It Up!

HAWAIIAN PIZZA

makes: 4 servings   hands-on time: 10 min.   total time: 20 min.

¾   **cup marinara sauce**

2   **(8-oz.) packages individual pizza crusts**

1   **cup diced smoked ham**

1   **cup chopped fresh pineapple**

¼   **cup diced green bell pepper**

½   **cup (2 oz.) shredded part-skim mozzarella cheese**

1. Preheat oven to 450°. Spread 3 Tbsp. marinara sauce over each of 4 individual pizza crusts. Top each with ¼ cup ham, ¼ cup pineapple, and 1 Tbsp. bell pepper. Sprinkle each with 2 Tbsp. cheese. Bake at 450° on middle oven rack 10 to 12 minutes.

Note: We tested with Natural Gourmet Kabuli Pizza Crust (2 per package).

Prep the toppings, and let kids "decorate" the pizzas with sauce, ham, pineapple, peppers, and cheese.

Little Helpers

---

serve with

CARROT-CUCUMBER SLAW

makes: 2 cups
hands-on time: 8 min.
total time: 8 min.

3   **Tbsp. fresh lime juice**

2   **tsp. olive oil**

¼   **cup chopped fresh mint**

¼   **cup chopped fresh cilantro**

½   **tsp. salt**

3   **large carrots**

1   **English cucumber**

1. Combine first 5 ingredients. Cut carrots and English cucumber into strips, using a julienne vegetable peeler or a mandoline. Toss with lime mixture; serve immediately.

SANTA FE PIZZA

makes: 4 servings   hands-on time: 8 min.   total time: 26 min.

This is an example of fusion cuisine kids will understand. An Italian pizza crust anchors south-of-the-border toppings in a family-friendly main dish.

½   (1-lb.) package ground mild or hot pork sausage

½   cup finely chopped red bell pepper

1   Tbsp. finely chopped pickled jalapeño pepper (optional)

1   (14-oz.) Italian pizza crust

1   cup chunky salsa

1   tsp. chili powder

½   cup canned black beans, drained and rinsed

1   cup (4 oz.) shredded Cheddar-Monterey Jack cheese blend

½   cup sour cream (optional)

Garnish: cilantro sprigs

1. Preheat oven to 450°. Cook sausage in a large skillet over medium-high heat, stirring until it crumbles and is no longer pink. Drain and pat dry with paper towels. Wipe skillet clean. Return sausage to skillet. Add bell pepper and jalapeño pepper, if desired; cook 3 minutes or until tender.

2. Place pizza crust on a baking sheet. Bake at 450° for 8 minutes. Combine salsa and chili powder; spread over warm crust. Top with sausage mixture and black beans; sprinkle with cheese.

3. Bake at 450° for 6 minutes or until cheese melts. Cut into 8 wedges. Serve with sour cream and garnish with cilantro, if desired.

Pizza Pointer

Cook sausage and peppers a day ahead. Keep refrigerated until ready to top and bake your pizza.

TWO-TOMATO TURKEY SAUSAGE PIZZA

makes: 6 servings   hands-on time: 10 min.   total time: 28 min.

1   lb. prepared pizza dough, at room temperature

Vegetable cooking spray

2   (4-oz.) links turkey Italian sausage, casings removed

1   Tbsp. oil from sun-dried tomatoes

4   oil-packed sun-dried tomatoes, drained

6   (0.67-oz.) slices provolone cheese

2   cups grape tomatoes, halved

Dried crushed red pepper (optional)

1. Preheat oven to 450°. While oven preheats, shape pizza dough into a 15½- x 10½-inch rectangle on a work surface; transfer to a large baking sheet coated with cooking spray. Place in oven on bottom rack while oven continues to preheat, and bake 10 minutes.

2. While crust prebakes, cook sausage in a skillet over medium-high heat until crumbly and no longer pink.

3. Remove crust from oven; rub with sun-dried tomato oil, and sprinkle with sun-dried tomatoes. Top with cheese, sausage, and grape tomato halves. Bake at 450° on bottom rack for 8 minutes or until crust is golden and cheese melts. Sprinkle with crushed red pepper before serving, if desired.

Pizza Pointer

Feel free to use whatever sausage you like in this recipe. A great option would be 8 oz. of spicy or regular ground sausage.

MEXICAN PIZZA

makes: 6 servings hands-on time: 20 min. total time: 40 min.

1 **(13.8-oz.) can refrigerated thin pizza crust dough**

½ **lb. sliced smoked chorizo sausage**

½ **cup thinly sliced sweet onion**

2 **tsp. olive oil**

4 **oz. cream cheese, softened**

1 **cup (4 oz.) shredded Monterey Jack cheese**

¼ **cup chopped fresh cilantro**

½ **tsp. lime zest**

1 **Tbsp. lime juice**

1½ **cups fresh corn kernels**

Fresh cilantro leaves

1. Preheat oven to 450°. Unroll dough; pat to an even thickness on a lightly greased baking sheet. Bake at 450° for 10 to 12 minutes or until lightly browned.

2. Sauté sausage and onion in hot olive oil until onion is tender; drain. Combine cream cheese, Monterey Jack cheese, cilantro, lime zest, and lime juice; spread over crust. Top with sausage mixture and corn kernels. Bake at 450° for 8 to 10 minutes. Sprinkle with fresh cilantro leaves.

Let kids help by spreading cream cheese mixture over crust and sprinkling with toppings. They'll be more likely to try new flavors if they helped make the pizza.

Little Helpers

serve with

ZIPPY BLACK BEANS

makes: 3 cups
hands-on time: 10 min.
total time: 10 min.

2 **(15-oz.) cans black beans, drained and rinsed**

1 **cup vegetable broth**

1 **small onion, chopped**

1 **jalapeño pepper, seeded and minced**

1 **Tbsp. olive oil**

1 **garlic clove, minced**

½ **tsp. salt**

1 **cup (4 oz.) shredded Mexican four-cheese blend**

1. Process black beans and vegetable broth in a food processor 10 to 15 seconds or until smooth. Sauté onion and jalapeño pepper in hot olive oil in a large skillet 4 to 5 minutes or until tender. Add garlic, and sauté 1 minute. Add black bean puree and salt, stirring until blended. Cook, stirring often, 3 minutes or until bean mixture is thoroughly heated. Stir in cheese until melted.

¡PIZZA FIESTA!

EASY GARLIC ROLLS

makes: 4 to 6 servings   hands-on time: 12 min.   total time: 20 min.

4   **bakery rolls**

½   **cup butter**

2   **garlic cloves, minced**

¼   **to ½ tsp. dried Italian seasoning**

PIZZA POINTER

We used Chicago-style hard rolls in this recipe. You could also use French bread rolls, a sliced French bread baguette, or any other small rolls from your grocery store.

1. Preheat oven to 400°. Cut rolls in half horizontally. Melt butter in a small saucepan over medium-low heat. Add minced garlic and dried Italian seasoning, and cook, stirring constantly, 1 to 2 minutes or until fragrant.

2. Brush butter mixture on cut sides of bread. Place bread, cut sides up, on a lightly greased baking sheet. Bake at 400° for 7 to 8 minutes or until lightly toasted.

PIZZERIA CLASSICS

These familiar favorites
taste like you've just ordered them
off the menu of your local pizzeria.

PIZZA MARGHERITA

makes: 5 servings hands-on time: 5 min. total time: 17 min.

Because this classic Neapolitan-style pizza is so simple, it depends on quality ingredients. Use the best fresh mozzarella and basil you can find.

1   (14-oz.) Italian pizza crust

½   cup Basic Pizza Sauce (page 9)

5   oz. fresh mozzarella cheese, thinly sliced

⅓   cup torn fresh basil leaves

1. Preheat oven to 450°.

2. Place pizza crust on a baking sheet. Spread Basic Pizza Sauce evenly over crust. Arrange cheese slices over sauce. Place on bottom rack of oven.

3. Bake at 450° for 12 minutes. Remove from oven, and sprinkle with basil. Serve immediately.

You can substitute jarred pizza sauce to speed up this recipe. Choose a tomato-basil or a spicy marinara for classic Italian flavor.

SPEED IT UP!

serve with
MIXED GREENS WITH GARLIC OIL DRESSING

makes: 8 cups
hands-on time: 5 min.
total time: 5 min.

2   garlic cloves, minced

2   tsp. chopped fresh oregano

½   tsp. freshly ground pepper

¼   tsp. salt

3   Tbsp. fresh lime juice

3   Tbsp. olive oil

2   (5-oz.) packages greens mix

1. Whisk together first 5 ingredients in a large bowl; add 2 Tbsp. water. Whisk in olive oil. Add spring greens mix, and toss gently to coat.

MOZZARELLA & BASIL MINI PIZZA

makes: 1 (6- to 8-inch) pizza hands-on time: 30 min. total time: 1 hour, 5 min.

This makes just one individual pizza, but you can double, triple, or even quadruple this recipe.

- **4** oz. prepared pizza dough, at room temperature
- **Parchment paper**
- **½** tsp. extra virgin olive oil
- **1** large plum tomato, thinly sliced
- **1** Tbsp. sliced fresh basil
- **4** thin slices (2 oz.) fresh mozzarella
- **1** (1-oz.) slice country ham or smoked ham, cut into thin strips
- **¼** tsp. freshly ground black pepper

PIZZA POINTER

Using a pizza stone isn't essential here, but it makes a better pizza. The hot stone crisps the crust from underneath, ensuring a perfectly cooked pizza from top to bottom.

1. Preheat oven to 450°. Shape dough into a 6- to 8-inch circle on a lightly floured surface. (Dough doesn't need to be perfectly round.) Place dough on a piece of parchment paper. Fold up edges of dough, forming a 1-inch border. Brush oil evenly over dough using a pastry brush.

2. Cover pizza dough circle loosely with plastic wrap, and let rise in a warm place (85°), free from drafts, 15 to 20 minutes.

3. Heat pizza stone or heavy baking sheet 10 to 12 minutes in oven. Remove and discard plastic wrap from dough. Layer tomato and next 3 ingredients evenly over dough. Sprinkle with pepper. Carefully transfer dough on parchment paper to pizza stone.

4. Bake at 450° for 10 minutes or until crust is golden.

FRESH TOMATO-FETA PIZZA

makes: 6 servings   hands-on time: 35 min.   total time: 55 min.

1   lb. refrigerated fresh pizza dough, at room temperature

Vegetable cooking spray

4   plum tomatoes, sliced

2½ Tbsp. olive oil, divided

2   garlic cloves, minced

Yellow cornmeal

4   oz. feta cheese

⅓   cup pitted kalamata olives, halved

¼   cup fresh basil leaves

1. Place dough in a bowl coated with cooking spray. Let dough stand, covered, 30 minutes or until dough comes to room temperature.

2. Arrange tomato slices on a jelly-roll pan lined with paper towels; top with more paper towels. Let stand 30 minutes.

3. Position oven rack in lowest setting. Place a pizza stone or heavy baking sheet on bottom rack in oven. Preheat oven to 500° (keep pizza stone or baking sheet in oven as it preheats). Preheat pizza stone or heavy baking sheet 30 minutes before baking pizza.

4. Combine tomatoes, 2 Tbsp. oil, and garlic. Sprinkle cornmeal on a lightly floured baking sheet without raised edges. Roll dough into a 14-inch circle on prepared baking sheet. Pierce dough liberally with a fork. Arrange tomato mixture over dough. Crumble cheese; sprinkle over pizza. Slide pizza onto preheated pizza stone or heavy baking sheet, using a spatula as a guide.

5. Bake at 500° for 19 minutes or until crust is golden and cheese is lightly browned. Remove from oven; top with olives and basil. Brush edges of crust with remaining 1½ tsp. oil.

Pizza Pointer

Draining the sliced tomatoes on paper towels keeps the crust from getting soggy.

GREAT GREEK FLAVOR!

ULTIMATE CHEESE PIZZA

makes: 4 servings hands-on time: 10 min. total time: 28 min.

Combine any leftover bits of cheese you find in the fridge for this simple pie.

1   (14.5-oz.) can whole tomatoes, drained and chopped

1   tsp. bottled minced garlic

1   (14-oz.) Italian pizza crust

2   cups (8 oz.) mixed shredded cheese

1. Preheat oven to 450°. Stir together tomatoes and garlic. Spread crust evenly with tomato mixture, and sprinkle with cheese.

2. Bake at 450° for 12 to 14 minutes or until cheese is melted.

Have kids choose the cheeses and shred them, then let them assemble this easy pizza.

Little Helpers

serve with
ROASTED BROCCOLI

makes: 6 servings
hands-on time: 6 min.
total time: 20 min.

1¼ lb. broccoli

1   Tbsp. olive oil

1   garlic clove, pressed

3   Tbsp. sliced almonds, toasted

1. Preheat oven to 475°.

2. Cut broccoli into 3-inch-long spears; cut thick stems in half lengthwise. Place in a single layer on a well-greased jelly-roll pan.

3. Combine olive oil and garlic; drizzle broccoli with oil mixture, and toss well. Sprinkle with salt and pepper to taste.

4. Bake at 475° for 14 minutes. Sprinkle almonds over broccoli.

PEPPERS-AND-CHEESE PIZZA

makes: 4 to 6 servings hands-on time: 25 min. total time: 43 min.

This combination of bell peppers and banana peppers pumps up the flavor in this tangy pizza with a kick.

1	medium onion, diced
1	medium-size green bell pepper, diced
1	large banana pepper, diced
3	garlic cloves, minced
¼	cup olive oil, divided
4	oz. cream cheese, softened
2	oz. feta cheese, crumbled
1	tsp. dried basil
1	tsp. dried oregano
1	tsp. dried sage
¼	tsp. salt
1	(13.8-oz.) can refrigerated pizza crust dough
½	cup shredded Parmesan cheese

1. Preheat oven to 400°. Sauté diced onion, diced peppers, and minced garlic in 2 Tbsp. olive oil in a large skillet over medium-high heat 5 minutes or until tender. Remove onion mixture from heat, and set aside.

2. Stir together cream cheese, next 5 ingredients, and remaining 2 Tbsp. olive oil until blended.

3. Place crust on a lightly greased baking sheet. Spread with cream cheese mixture; sprinkle with onion mixture and Parmesan cheese.

4. Bake at 400° for 15 to 18 minutes or until cheese is melted.

This pizza uses a lot of fresh garlic. To save time, use 2 tsp. jarred minced garlic instead of chopping your own. Or, use a garlic press to make quick work of the fresh garlic cloves.

SPEED IT UP!

ULTIMATE VEGGIE PIZZA

makes: 4 servings   hands-on time: 10 min.   total time: 24 min.

Grilled vegetables such as yellow squash, zucchini, bell pepper, and onions make a great side dish for grilled meats or on their own as a meatless main dish.

2 cups Grilled Summer Veggies	1 (14-oz.) Italian pizza crust
1 (14.5-oz.) can whole tomatoes, drained and chopped	2 cups (8 oz.) mixed shredded cheese
1 tsp. bottled minced garlic	

1. Preheat oven to 450°. Prepare Grilled Summer Veggies.

2. Stir together tomatoes and garlic. Spread crust evenly with tomato mixture, and sprinkle with cheese; arrange vegetables over cheese.

3. Bake at 450° for 12 to 14 minutes or until cheese is melted.

GRILLED SUMMER VEGGIES

makes: 6 servings
hands-on time: 20 min.
total time: 20 min.

2   medium-size red bell peppers, cut into 1-inch-thick slices

3   medium-size yellow squash, cut into ¼-inch-thick slices

3   small zucchini, cut into ¼-inch-thick slices

2   medium-size sweet onions, cut into ½-inch-thick slices

Vegetable cooking spray

½   tsp. salt

½   tsp. pepper

1. Preheat grill to 350° to 400° (medium-high) heat. Lightly coat vegetables evenly with cooking spray.

2. Grill vegetables, covered with grill lid, 3 to 5 minutes on each side or until tender. Remove from grill, and sprinkle evenly with salt and pepper.

CARAMELIZED ONION & MUSHROOM PIZZA

makes: 4 to 6 servings hands-on time: 29 min. total time: 41 min.

The extra time it takes to caramelize the onions before adding to this pizza is well worth it. A little balsamic vinegar and cremini mushrooms take this pizza over the top.

1   large sweet onion, cut into ¼-inch slices

2   Tbsp. olive oil, divided

2   Tbsp. butter, divided

1½   Tbsp. balsamic vinegar

1   (8-oz.) package cremini mushrooms, sliced

½   tsp. salt

¼   tsp. freshly ground pepper

2   large garlic cloves, minced

1   Tbsp. chopped fresh oregano

1   Tbsp. chopped fresh thyme

1   lb. prepared pizza dough, at room temperature

Yellow cornmeal

1½   (8-oz.) blocks mozzarella cheese, shredded and divided

¼   cup (1 oz.) shredded Parmesan cheese

1. Preheat oven to 450°. Heat pizza stone according to manufacturer's instructions.

2. Separate onion slices into rings. Heat 1 Tbsp. oil and 1 Tbsp. butter in a large nonstick skillet over medium heat until butter melts. Add onion, and cook 15 minutes or until onion is caramelized, stirring occasionally. Stir in balsamic vinegar, and cook, stirring constantly, 2 minutes. Remove from heat.

3. Meanwhile, heat remaining 1 Tbsp. oil and 1 Tbsp. butter in a large skillet over medium-high heat until butter melts. Add mushrooms and next 3 ingredients. Cook until mushrooms are browned and liquid evaporates, stirring occasionally. Remove from heat; stir in oregano and thyme.

4. Roll dough into a 12-inch circle on a lightly floured surface. Sprinkle cornmeal on preheated stone; place dough on stone. Bake at 450° for 10 minutes.

5. Sprinkle 1 cup mozzarella cheese on pizza crust; top with onion and mushroom mixtures. Sprinkle remaining 2 cups mozzarella cheese and Parmesan cheese over vegetables. Bake 5 more minutes or until crust is golden brown and cheese melts.

HAVE-IT-YOUR-WAY PIZZA

makes: 4 servings hands-on time: 12 min. total time: 25 min.

Here's a pizza that delivers just what the kids want on half the crust—a thin layer of pizza sauce and lots of gooey cheese, while the other side has a little extra for the more adventurous.

2   tsp. olive oil

1   (13.8-oz.) can refrigerated pizza crust dough

2   plum tomatoes

8   pitted kalamata or other black olives

¼   small red onion

⅔   cup pizza sauce

2   oz. crumbled feta cheese with basil and sun-dried tomato

1   cup (4 oz.) shredded Cheddar-mozzarella cheese blend

1. Preheat oven to 425°. Brush oil over pizza crust; place on an ungreased baking sheet. Bake at 425° for 5 minutes.

2. Meanwhile, thinly slice tomatoes, halve olives, and thinly slice onion.

3. Remove crust from oven; spread pizza sauce over pizza crust, leaving a 1-inch margin. Arrange tomato, olives, and onion over half of pizza; sprinkle with feta cheese. Sprinkle Cheddar-mozzarella cheese over remaining half of pizza.

4. Bake at 425° for 8 minutes or just until cheese melts.

serve with
BELL PEPPER PASTA SALAD

makes: 4 cups
hands-on time: 5 min.
total time: 15 min.

2   cups farfalle (bow-tie) pasta

2   Tbsp. white balsamic vinegar

1   Tbsp. olive oil

⅛   tsp. salt

⅛   tsp. freshly ground pepper

½   cup refrigerated prechopped tricolor bell pepper mix

1   Tbsp. chopped fresh dill

1. Cook pasta according to package directions.

2. While pasta cooks, combine white balsamic vinegar, olive oil, salt, and freshly ground black pepper in a medium bowl, stirring with a whisk.

3. Add pasta, bell pepper mix, and chopped fresh dill; toss well.

PEPPERONI PIZZA

makes: 6 servings   hands-on time: 5 min.   total time: 17 min.

If you're looking for a super-simple, quick pizza, this is it!

1	**cup tomato-and-basil pasta sauce**
1	**(14-oz.) Italian pizza crust**
1	**(3.5-oz.) package pepperoni slices**
1½	**cups (6 oz.) part-skim mozzarella cheese**

1. Preheat oven to 450°. Spoon pasta sauce evenly over crust, leaving a 1-inch border around edges. Top with half of pepperoni slices. Sprinkle with cheese. Top with remaining pepperoni.

2. Bake pizza at 450° directly on oven rack 11 to 12 minutes or until crust is golden and cheese is melted. Serve immediately.

Let kids make this pizza their work of art by arranging pepperoni in a fun pattern or smiley face.

Little Helpers

serve with

ROMAINE SALAD

makes: 4 cups
hands-on time: 8 min.
total time: 8 min.

⅓	**cup fresh lemon juice**
1	**tsp. Worcestershire sauce**
2	**garlic cloves, pressed**
¾	**tsp. kosher salt**
½	**tsp. freshly ground pepper**
½	**cup olive oil**
1	**head romaine lettuce, torn**
½	**cup freshly grated or shredded Parmesan cheese**
1	**cup large plain croutons**

1. Whisk together first 5 ingredients. Whisk in olive oil.

2. Place romaine lettuce in a large bowl. Pour olive oil mixture over lettuce, and toss.

3. Sprinkle with freshly grated or shredded Parmesan cheese, tossing to combine. Top with croutons, and serve immediately.

PEPPERONI, ONION & OLIVE PIZZA

makes: 6 servings hands-on time: 7 min. total time: 54 min.

This classic pizza gets jazzed up by adding olives and thinly sliced sweet onion to the pepperoni.

Yellow cornmeal

1 **lb. prepared pizza dough, at room temperature**

½ **cup lower-sodium marinara sauce**

½ **cup thinly sliced sweet onion**

1 **oz. pepperoni slices (about 18 slices)**

10 **pitted niçoise olives, halved lengthwise**

¾ **cup (3 oz.) shredded reduced-fat Italian four-cheese blend**

1. Position oven rack in lowest setting. Preheat oven to 450°. Sprinkle a baking sheet with cornmeal; roll dough into a 12-inch circle on prepared baking sheet.

2. Spread sauce evenly over dough, leaving a ½-inch border. Top with onion, pepperoni, and olives; sprinkle with cheese.

3. Bake at 450° on bottom rack in oven 17 minutes or until crust is golden.

Pizza Pointer

By baking this pizza on the bottom rack of a hot oven, you're ensured a crispy crust.

WHOLE WHEAT PEPPERONI PIZZA

makes: 6 servings   hands-on time: 5 min.   total time: 16 min.

Pepperoni pizza is a classic favorite, and in less than 20 minutes, you can make this light and healthy version.

1   lb. prepared whole wheat pizza dough, at room temperature

Vegetable cooking spray

⅔   cup tomato-basil pasta sauce

24   slices turkey pepperoni

1½   cups (6 oz.) part-skim mozzarella cheese

1. Preheat oven to 500°. Roll dough into a 12-inch circle. Place dough on an inverted large baking sheet coated with cooking spray. Crimp edges of dough to form a rim. Spread sauce over surface of dough, leaving a ½-inch border; sprinkle sauce with pepperoni and cheese.

2. Bake at 500° for 11 minutes or until cheese melts and crust is golden.

serve with
MANDARIN ORANGE SALAD

makes: 4 cups
hands-on time: 5 min.
total time: 5 min.

1   (5-oz.) head Bibb lettuce

½   cup mandarin oranges, drained

¼   cup candied almonds

¼   cup bottled ginger dressing

1. Toss together first 3 ingredients. Serve with bottled ginger dressing.

BEEF & PEPPERONI PIZZA

makes: 4 servings hands-on time: 2 min. total time: 15 min.

We reduced the fat, calories, and sodium in this pizzeria-style meat pizza by opting for lighter turkey pepperoni. This trims the fat by 50 percent and still delivers the zesty, spicy flavor of regular pepperoni.

1   (10-oz.) whole wheat thin pizza crust

Olive oil–flavored cooking spray

½   lb. extra lean ground beef

1   (8-oz.) package sliced mushrooms

¾   cup marinara sauce

¾   oz. turkey pepperoni (about 12 slices)

⅔   cup (about 2.7 oz.) shredded part-skim mozzarella cheese

¼   tsp. dried crushed red pepper

1. Preheat oven to 450°. Place pizza crust on rack in oven while oven pre-heats; heat 5 minutes.

2. While crust heats, heat a large nonstick skillet over medium-high heat. Coat pan with cooking spray. Add beef and mushrooms; sauté 5 minutes or until beef crumbles and is no longer pink. Drain.

3. Remove crust from oven; place on an ungreased baking sheet. Coat crust with cooking spray; spread marinara sauce over crust, leaving a 1-inch border. Top with beef mixture, pepperoni, and cheese. Sprinkle evenly with red pepper.

4. Bake at 450° for 7 to 10 minutes or until crust is golden and cheese melts. Serve immediately.

BEEF & BACON PIZZA

makes: 8 servings   hands-on time: 20 min.   total time: 45 min.

This meat-lover's pizza is equally pleasing for a family dinner or for a casual party.

½   **lb. lean ground beef**

1¼ **cups sliced onion**

3   **garlic cloves, minced**

1   **tsp. chopped fresh rosemary**

½   **tsp. freshly ground black pepper**

Yellow cornmeal

1   **lb. prepared pizza dough, at room temperature**

½   **cup marinara sauce**

1   **cup (4 oz.) part-skim mozzarella cheese, shredded and divided**

½   **cup (2 oz.) freshly grated Parmesan cheese**

4   **slices center-cut bacon, cooked and crumbled**

PIZZA POINTER

Preshredded cheeses don't melt as easily as freshly grated cheeses from a block, so it's worth it to do it yourself.

1. Preheat oven to 450°. Cook beef in a large nonstick skillet over medium-high heat until beef crumbles and is no longer pink. Drain. Add onion to pan; sauté 6 minutes or until tender and beginning to brown. Add garlic; sauté 1 minute. Add beef, rosemary, and pepper to onion mixture.

2. Sprinkle cornmeal on a large baking sheet. Roll dough into a 12-inch circle; place on prepared baking sheet. Spread sauce over dough, leaving a ½-inch border. Sprinkle with ½ cup mozzarella cheese. Spread beef mixture over cheese. Top with remaining mozzarella and Parmesan cheeses. Sprinkle with bacon.

3. Bake at 450° for 15 minutes or until crust is golden.

BACON, ONION & MUSHROOM PIZZA

makes: 6 servings hands-on time: 23 min. total time: 38 min.

---

1 Tbsp. olive oil, divided

2 cups vertically sliced onion (about 2 small)

1 (8-oz.) package sliced cremini mushrooms

Yellow cornmeal

1 (11-oz.) can refrigerated French bread dough

1 cup (4 oz.) shredded white Cheddar cheese

6 bacon slices, cooked and coarsely crumbled

¼ cup finely chopped fresh flat-leaf parsley (optional)

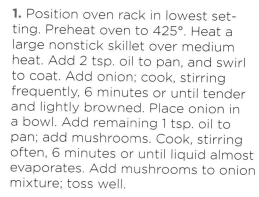

This recipe is made quick by using refrigerated French bread dough. Carefully unroll the dough, starting with the seam along the side.

1. Position oven rack in lowest setting. Preheat oven to 425°. Heat a large nonstick skillet over medium heat. Add 2 tsp. oil to pan, and swirl to coat. Add onion; cook, stirring frequently, 6 minutes or until tender and lightly browned. Place onion in a bowl. Add remaining 1 tsp. oil to pan; add mushrooms. Cook, stirring often, 6 minutes or until liquid almost evaporates. Add mushrooms to onion mixture; toss well.

2. Sprinkle cornmeal on a large baking sheet. Gently unroll dough onto a lightly floured surface. Roll dough into an 11-inch circle; transfer to prepared pan. Spread onion mixture over prepared dough to within ¼ inch of edge. Sprinkle onion mixture with cheese and bacon. Place pan on bottom rack in oven.

3. Bake at 425° for 15 minutes or until crust is golden. Sprinkle with parsley, if desired.

SAUSAGE PIZZA

makes: 8 servings hands-on time: 19 min. total time: 49 min.

The combination of Italian sausage, fennel, and red onion blends pleasant spicy heat with intriguing anise flavor for a complex-tasting pizza.

1½ tsp. olive oil

¼ to ½ tsp. dried crushed red pepper

1 (4-oz.) link sweet turkey Italian sausage, casing removed

½ cup vertically sliced fennel bulb

½ cup thinly vertically sliced red onion (about 1 small onion)

¼ tsp. kosher salt

⅔ cup chopped seeded tomato (about 2 tomatoes)

1 lb. prepared pizza dough, at room temperature

Vegetable cooking spray

¼ cup (1 oz.) freshly grated Parmigiano-Reggiano cheese

1. Position oven rack in lowest setting. Place a pizza stone or heavy baking sheet on bottom rack in oven. Preheat oven to 500° (keep pizza stone or baking sheet in oven as it preheats). Preheat pizza stone or heavy baking sheet 30 minutes before baking pizza.

2. Heat oil in a large nonstick skillet over medium-high heat. Add pepper to pan; cook 10 seconds. Add sausage, fennel, and onion to pan; sauté 4 minutes or until sausage crumbles and is no longer pink. Stir in salt. Add tomato; sauté 2 minutes or until tender. Remove from heat.

3. Roll dough into a 10-inch circle on a lightly floured surface. Place dough on a 10-inch pizza pan or baking sheet coated with cooking spray.

4. Spread sausage mixture over dough, leaving a ½-inch border. Slide dough onto preheated pizza stone or heavy baking sheet, using a spatula as a guide.

5. Bake at 500° for 8 minutes or until crust is golden. Sprinkle with cheese.

CARNE LOVER'S PIZZA

makes: 8 servings hands-on time: 10 min. total time: 2 hours, 12 min.

1 lb. prepared pizza dough, at room temperature

1 medium-size yellow onion, cut vertically into thin slices

1 lb. mild Italian sausage, casings removed

2 Tbsp. olive oil

6 (1-oz.) mozzarella cheese slices

6 cooked bacon slices, crumbled

2 oz. thin pepperoni slices (about 28 slices)

½ cup chopped Canadian bacon slices (5 slices)

1½ cups Spicy Tomato Pizza Sauce (page 10)

1. Let pizza dough stand, covered, at room temperature 1 hour.

2. Meanwhile, cook onion and sausage in a large skillet over medium-high heat, stirring often, 8 minutes or until sausage crumbles and is no longer pink; drain.

3. Brush a 12-inch cast-iron skillet with oil. Press dough on bottom and up sides of skillet. Cover dough loosely with plastic wrap, and let rise in a warm place (85°), free from drafts, 30 minutes. Press dough up sides of skillet.

4. Preheat oven to 450°. Bake crust at 450° for 6 minutes or until crust is set and beginning to brown. Remove skillet from oven. Lay cheese slices on top of crust, slightly overlapping. Layer sausage mixture, bacon, pepperoni, and Canadian bacon over cheese. Spread pizza sauce over meats.

5. Bake at 450° for 18 to 20 minutes or until crust is golden.

Pick up a jar of spicy marinara to substitute for the homemade sauce, if you're in a hurry.

SPEED IT UP!

ITALIAN SAUSAGE DEEP-DISH PIZZA

makes: 4 servings hands-on time: 15 min. total time: 1 hour, 30 min.

½ (32-oz.) package frozen bread dough

Yellow cornmeal

9 oz. Italian sausage, casings removed

1 cup chunky spaghetti sauce or pizza sauce

½ cup sliced fresh mushrooms

⅓ cup sliced black olives

1 cup (4 oz.) shredded mozzarella cheese

1. Thaw bread dough according to package directions. Press dough into a lightly greased 12-inch deep-dish pizza pan covered with cornmeal. Let dough rise in a warm place (85°), free from drafts, for 30 minutes.

2. Preheat oven to 400°. Brown sausage in a small skillet over medium heat, stirring until sausage crumbles and is no longer pink. Drain on paper towels.

3. Press dough down in center, leaving a 1½-inch edge.

4. Bake on lower oven rack at 400° for 5 minutes. Spread spaghetti sauce in center of crust; sprinkle with sausage, mushrooms, and olives. Top with cheese. Bake at 400° for 10 to 12 minutes.

serve with

SAUTÉED ZUCCHINI & BELL PEPPER

makes: 2 cups
hands-on time: 10 min.
total time: 10 min.

1 medium zucchini, cut into 2-inch pieces

1 cup refrigerated chopped green, red, and yellow bell pepper

1 garlic clove, minced

¼ tsp. salt

1 tsp. hot oil

1. Sauté first 4 ingredients in hot oil in a large nonstick skillet over medium-high heat 7 minutes.

"THE WORKS" PIZZA

makes: 6 servings hands-on time: 20 min. total time: 50 min.

2 tsp. olive oil, divided

¼ lb. ground sausage

1 cup chopped red bell pepper (about 1 small)

1 cup sliced fresh mushrooms

½ cup finely chopped onion (about 1 small)

1 small garlic clove, minced

¼ cup sliced, drained black olives

Vegetable cooking spray

1 lb. prepared pizza dough, at room temperature

Yellow cornmeal

¾ cup pizza sauce

1½ cups (6 oz.) shredded part-skim mozzarella cheese

1. Preheat oven to 450°. Heat 1 tsp. olive oil in a heavy medium skillet over medium heat. Cook sausage in hot oil 5 minutes or until sausage crumbles and is no longer pink. Add bell pepper, mushrooms, and onion; cook 4 minutes or until vegetables are tender, stirring occasionally. Add garlic; sauté 1 minute. Stir in olives; drain sausage mixture on paper towels.

2. Coat a 12-inch pizza pan with cooking spray. Place dough on pan; sprinkle with cornmeal to prevent sticking to fingers. Press dough onto pan; crimp edges of dough with fingers to form a rim. Place on bottom rack of oven.

3. Bake at 450° for 10 minutes. Remove from oven, and brush edges of crust with remaining 1 tsp. olive oil. Spread pizza sauce evenly over crust. Top with sausage mixture and cheese. Place on middle rack of oven. Bake at 450° for 15 minutes.

Pizza Pointer

Draining the cooked sausage mixture is an important step in this recipe; if you skip it, your pizza will turn out greasy.

PIZZA SUPREME

makes: 6 servings hands-on time: 21 min. total time: 35 min.

Brighten a homemade version of a take-out favorite with two different colors of bell peppers. Orange bell peppers impart a tangy fruity flavor, while red peppers are sweet and juicy additions to your pizza.

1   lb. prepared pizza dough, at room temperature

Vegetable cooking spray

2   tsp. olive oil

1   (4-oz.) link sweet turkey Italian sausage, casing removed

1   cup sliced fresh mushrooms

1   cup thinly sliced red bell pepper

1   cup thinly sliced orange bell pepper

1   cup thinly sliced red onion

¼   tsp. dried crushed red pepper

3   garlic cloves, thinly sliced

¾   cup lower-sodium marinara sauce

5   oz. fresh mozzarella cheese, thinly sliced

1. Preheat oven to 500°.

2. Roll dough into a 14-inch circle on a lightly floured surface. Place dough on a 14-inch pizza pan or baking sheet coated with cooking spray.

3. Heat oil in a large nonstick skillet over medium-high heat. Add sausage to pan; cook 2 minutes or until sausage crumbles and is no longer pink. Add mushrooms, bell peppers, onion, crushed red pepper, and garlic; sauté 4 minutes, stirring occasionally. Drain.

4. Spread sauce over dough, leaving a 1-inch border. Arrange cheese over sauce. Arrange sausage mixture evenly over cheese. Bake at 500° for 15 minutes or until crust and cheese are browned.

CHICAGO DEEP-DISH PIZZA

makes: 8 servings   hands-on time: 30 min.   total time: 1 hour, 10 min.

1   lb. prepared pizza dough, at room temperature

Vegetable cooking spray

2   cups (8 oz.) shredded part-skim mozzarella cheese, divided

2   precooked mild Italian chicken sausages (about 6 oz.), casings removed, chopped

1   (28-oz.) can whole tomatoes, drained

1½   tsp. chopped fresh oregano

1½   tsp. chopped fresh basil

1   tsp. olive oil

2   cups thinly sliced mushrooms (about 6 oz.)

¾   cup chopped green bell pepper

¾   cup chopped red bell pepper

1. Roll dough into an 15- x 11-inch rectangle on a lightly floured surface. Place dough in a 13- x 9-inch glass or ceramic baking dish coated with cooking spray; press dough up sides of dish. Spread 1½ cups cheese evenly over dough. Arrange chopped sausage evenly over cheese.

2. Preheat oven to 400°. Chop tomatoes; place in a sieve. Stir in oregano and basil; drain tomato mixture 10 minutes.

3. Heat 1 tsp. olive oil in a large non-stick skillet over medium heat. Add mushrooms; cook 5 minutes, stirring occasionally. Stir in bell peppers; cook 8 minutes or until tender, stirring occasionally. Arrange vegetables over sausage; spoon tomato mixture evenly over vegetables and sausage. Sprinkle evenly with remaining ½ cup cheese.

4. Bake at 400° for 25 minutes or until crust is golden and cheese bubbles.

OH-SO CHEESY!

ANTIPASTO PIZZA

makes: 4 servings hands-on time: 10 min. total time: 24 min.

Roasted or marinated vegetables, such as red bell peppers, assorted olives, or pickled okra, would also taste great on this zesty pie.

- 1 **(14-oz.) Italian pizza crust**
- ¼ **cup refrigerated light pesto sauce**
- ¾ **cup chopped artichoke hearts**
- ½ **cup diced salami or deli ham**
- ¼ **cup sliced banana peppers**
- ¼ **cup sliced black olives**
- ¼ **cup sun-dried tomatoes in oil, drained and chopped**
- 1½ **cups (6 oz.) shredded mozzarella cheese**

1. Preheat oven to 450°. Spread pizza crust evenly with pesto. Sprinkle evenly with artichoke hearts and next 4 ingredients. Sprinkle with cheese.

2. Bake at 450° for 12 to 14 minutes or until cheese is melted.

serve with
GRAPEFRUIT SALAD

makes: 6 cups
hands-on time: 5 min.
total time: 5 min.

- 1 **(5-oz.) package mixed salad greens**
- 2 **cups refrigerated red grapefruit sections**
- 2 **cups sliced avocado**
- ½ **cup sweetened dried cranberries**
- ⅓ **cup bottled poppy-seed dressing**

1. Toss together all ingredients. Serve immediately.

VEGETARIAN STROMBOLI

makes: 6 servings hands-on time: 21 min. total time: 33 min.

"Meaty" Filling

Olive oil–flavored cooking spray

1 (11-oz.) can refrigerated thin pizza crust dough

1½ Tbsp. prepared mustard

5 (⅔-oz.) reduced-fat provolone cheese slices

1. Preheat oven to 425°.

2. Prepare "Meaty" Filling. Cover and chill until ready to make stromboli.

3. Coat a baking sheet with cooking spray. Unroll dough onto a large baking sheet; press into a 12- x 8-inch rectangle. Thinly spread mustard over dough to within ½ inch of edges. Spread "Meaty" Filling lengthwise down center third of dough, leaving a 1-inch border at both ends. Top filling with cheese.

4. Cut slits from edge of filling to edge of dough at 1-inch intervals on long sides of rectangle. Alternating sides, fold strips at an angle across filling. Coat top of dough with cooking spray.

5. Bake at 425° for 12 minutes or until browned.

"MEATY" FILLING

makes: 6 servings
hands-on time: 6 min.
total time: 6 min.

Olive oil–flavored cooking spray

1 cup frozen vegetarian meatless crumbles

½ cup chopped red onion

½ cup tomato-and-basil pasta sauce

¼ cup sliced black olives

¼ cup thinly sliced fresh basil

1. Heat a large nonstick skillet over medium-high heat. Coat pan with cooking spray. Add meatless crumbles and onion to pan; sauté 3 minutes or until onion is tender. Stir in pasta sauce and remaining ingredients.

Note: We tested with Morningstar Farms Meal Starters.

If braiding dough across the top is too fussy, just roll up the dough starting at one long side. Tuck the ends under, and pinch to seal. Then cut three or four slits (steam vents) across the top of the dough.

Speed It Up!

A FUN "TWIST" ON PIZZA!

BROCCOLI-CHEESE CALZONES

makes: 4 servings   hands-on time: 20 min.   total time: 35 min.

These cheesy calzones with mushrooms and broccoli are a great vegetarian meal. If you're craving something a little heartier, try the Beef Calzones variation below.

Parchment paper

1   tsp. olive oil

1   cup broccoli florets

1   cup sliced mushrooms

¼   tsp. dried crushed red pepper

1   lb. prepared pizza dough, at room temperature

1   cup (4 oz.) shredded part-skim mozzarella cheese

Vegetable cooking spray

1   cup pizza sauce, warmed (optional)

1. Preheat oven to 375°.

2. Line a baking sheet with parchment paper. Set aside.

3. Heat a large nonstick skillet over medium-high heat. Add oil, swirling to coat pan. Add broccoli, mushrooms, and red pepper; sauté 5 minutes or until lightly browned and moisture evaporates. Remove from heat.

4. Cut dough into 4 equal portions. Roll 1 portion into a 6-inch circle on a lightly floured surface. Repeat procedure with remaining dough.

5. Spoon ¼ cup vegetable filling into center of each circle; sprinkle each with ¼ cup cheese. Brush edges of dough with water; fold dough in half over filling, pressing firmly to seal.

6. Place calzones on prepared baking sheet; coat tops with cooking spray. Bake at 375° for 15 minutes or until crust is golden brown. Cool slightly, and serve with warm pizza sauce, if desired.

Beef Calzones: Replace the vegetable filling with a meaty version. Starting with step 3, cook ½ lb. ground sirloin, ½ cup chopped onion, 1 tsp. onion powder, 1 tsp. garlic powder, 1 tsp. dried Italian seasoning, and 2 minced garlic cloves in a large nonstick skillet over medium-high heat 5 minutes, or until meat crumbles and is no longer pink. Drain. Proceed with recipe as directed.

SPINACH & BEEF CALZONES

makes: 6 servings   hands-on time: 30 min.   total time: 1 hour

1   lb. lean ground beef

3½ cups (14 oz.) shredded mozzarella cheese, divided

1   (6-oz.) can low-sodium tomato paste

½   cup frozen chopped spinach, thawed and drained

2   tsp. dried Italian seasoning

2   (13.8-oz.) cans refrigerated pizza crust dough

Olive oil

1½ cups jarred pasta sauce

Pizza Pointer

Freeze baked calzones for an easy weeknight dinner. To reheat, wrap calzones in aluminum foil, and bake at 300° for 1 hour or until throughly heated.

1. Preheat oven to 375°. Cook ground beef in a large skillet over medium-high heat, stirring until it crumbles and is no longer pink. Drain.

2. Combine beef, 2½ cups cheese, and next 3 ingredients.

3. Unroll each pizza crust, and cut each crust into thirds. Roll each portion into a 5-inch circle. Spread ¾ cup meat mixture evenly over half of each circle. Moisten edges with water; fold dough over, pressing or crimping edges to seal. Place on a lightly greased baking sheet, and cut slits in tops to allow steam to escape. Brush with olive oil.

4. Bake at 375° for 25 to 30 minutes or until golden. Top with pasta sauce; sprinkle with remaining cheese. Melt cheese under broiler, if desired.

Chicken Alfredo Calzones:
Replace the beef with ground chicken and the pasta sauce with jarred Alfredo sauce. Proceed with recipe as directed.

CHEESY PEPPERONI CALZONES

makes: 4 servings hands-on time: 20 min. total time: 45 min.

1   cup small-curd cottage cheese

3   Tbsp. grated Parmesan cheese

1   large egg

1   Tbsp. chopped fresh parsley or 1 tsp. dried parsley flakes

½   tsp. garlic powder

1   (3.5-oz.) package pepperoni slices, chopped

4   (¾-oz.) Monterey Jack cheese slices, chopped

2   (11-oz.) cans refrigerated thin pizza crust dough

½   (24-oz.) jar pasta sauce, warmed

1. Preheat oven to 375°. Stir together first 5 ingredients until blended. Stir in pepperoni and chopped cheese slices.

2. Divide each pizza crust into 2 portions. Roll each dough portion into a 7-inch circle.

3. Spoon ½ cup cottage cheese mixture in center of each circle. Fold dough over filling, pressing edges to seal with tines of a fork; place on a lightly greased aluminum foil-lined baking sheet. Cut 3 large slits in the dough.

4. Bake at 375° for 20 to 25 minutes or until golden. Let stand 5 minutes. Serve calzones with warm pasta sauce.

serve with
ROASTED VEGETABLES

makes: 5 cups
hands-on time: 10 min.
total time: 40 min.

3   sweet potatoes (about 1½ lb.), cut into ½-inch cubes

1   yellow bell pepper, cut into 1-inch pieces

1   medium onion, coarsely chopped

2   Tbsp. olive oil

1   tsp. salt

1   tsp. ground cinnamon

¼   tsp. pepper

1. Preheat oven to 450°.

2. Combine all ingredients in a large zip-top plastic freezer bag; seal bag, and turn until vegetables are coated. Remove vegetable mixture from bag, and place in a single layer in a lightly greased 15- x 10-inch jelly-roll pan.

3. Bake at 450° for 30 to 35 minutes or until sweet potatoes are tender.

CARAMELIZED ONION FLATBREAD

makes: 8 servings hands-on time: 25 min. total time: 45 min.

1 large sweet onion, sliced

3 Tbsp. olive oil, divided

1 lb. prepared pizza dough, at room temperature

1¼ tsp. kosher salt

1 tsp. chopped fresh rosemary

1. Preheat oven to 425°. Sauté onion in 1 Tbsp. hot oil over medium-high heat 15 minutes or until golden brown.

2. Press dough into a 15- x 10-inch jelly-roll pan, pressing to about ¼-inch thickness. Press handle of a wooden spoon into dough to make indentations at 1-inch intervals; drizzle with remaining 2 Tbsp. oil, and sprinkle with salt, rosemary, and caramelized onions.

3. Bake at 425° on lowest oven rack 20 minutes or until lightly browned.

PIZZA POINTER

If you can't find prepared pizza dough, you can use a (13.8-oz.) can of refrigerated pizza crust dough. Just reduce the salt to ¾ tsp. and reduce the bake time to 10 minutes or until lightly browned.

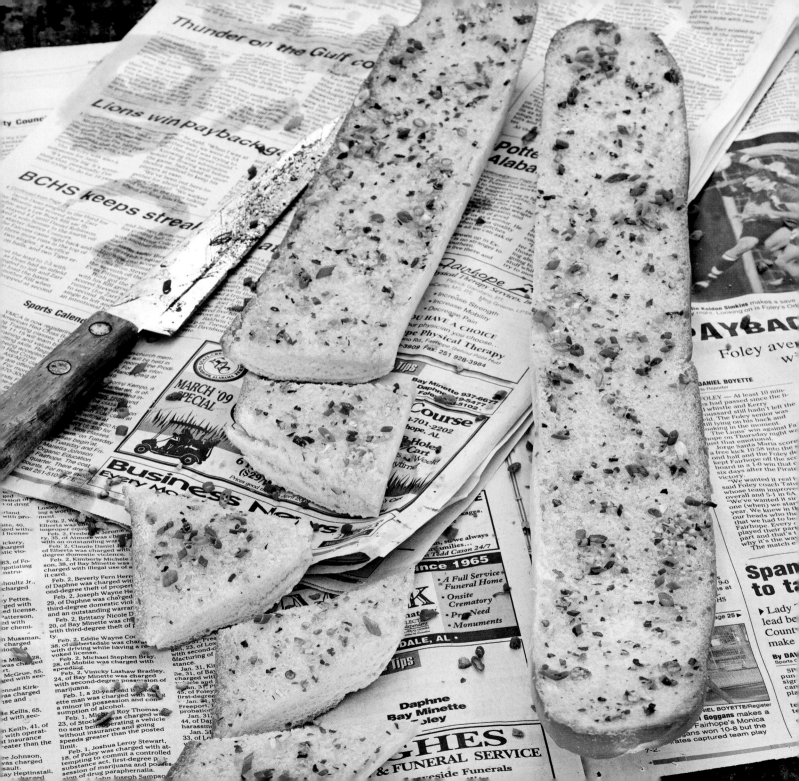

GARLIC-HERB BREAD

makes: 8 servings   hands-on time: 10 min.   total time: 25 min.

3   garlic cloves, minced

2   Tbsp. extra virgin olive oil

2   Tbsp. butter, melted

1   Tbsp. chopped fresh chives

½   tsp. dried crushed red pepper

1   (16-oz.) French bread loaf

1. Preheat oven to 350°. Stir together first 5 ingredients in a small bowl.

2. Cut bread in half lengthwise. Brush cut sides with garlic mixture; place on a baking sheet.

3. Bake at 350° for 13 to 15 minutes or until golden brown. Cut each bread half into 8 slices.

Kids can help by brushing the butter mixture over the cut sides of the bread—just keep some paper towels handy!

Little Helpers

FRESH LEMON GREENS ON RED PEPPER FOCACCIA

makes: 4 servings hands-on time: 10 min. total time: 29 min.

This knife-and-fork combination is a meal in one with salad greens, fresh vegetables, and warm bread.

1   (13.8-oz.) can refrigerated pizza crust dough

Vegetable cooking spray

1¼ cups red bell pepper strips (about 1 medium)

¼   cup (1 oz.) crumbled reduced-fat feta cheese with basil and sun-dried tomatoes

2   tsp. olive oil

1   Tbsp. lemon juice

1   tsp. dried basil

1   tsp. Dijon mustard

½   tsp. bottled minced garlic

¼   tsp. dried crushed red pepper

5   cups gourmet salad greens

¾   cup grape or cherry tomatoes, halved

⅓   cup thinly sliced red onion

1. Preheat oven to 400°. Unroll pizza dough; place on a baking sheet coated with cooking spray. Press into a 13- x 9-inch rectangle. Arrange bell pepper strips in a single layer over crust.

2. Bake 19 minutes at 400° or until crust is lightly browned. Remove from oven and immediately sprinkle with feta cheese.

3. While crust is baking, combine olive oil and next 5 ingredients in a small bowl; stir with a whisk. Combine salad greens, tomatoes, and onion in a large bowl. Pour dressing over salad; toss gently.

4. Cut focaccia into 4 rectangles; top each focaccia rectangle evenly with greens. Serve immediately.

PIZZAS with PIZZAZZ!

Prepare to be "wowed"
with the delicious and surprising
flavor combinations in these pizzas.

LOCAL FARMERS' MARKET PIZZA

makes: 6 servings   hands-on time: 28 min.   total time: 56 min.

Summer's best produce—including plump corn, crisp bell peppers, fragrant herbs, and sweet tomatoes—comes together to make this pizza a fun way to enjoy veggies.

1   Tbsp. extra virgin olive oil

2   cups thinly sliced onion

1   tsp. chopped fresh thyme

2   cups thinly sliced red bell pepper

5   garlic cloves, thinly sliced

1   cup fresh corn kernels (about 2 ears)

¼   tsp. freshly ground black pepper

¼   tsp. salt

1   lb. prepared pizza dough, at room temperature

Vegetable cooking spray

5   oz. thinly sliced fresh mozzarella cheese

⅓   cup (1½ oz.) grated Parmigiano-Reggiano cheese

1   cup cherry tomatoes, halved

⅓ cup fresh basil leaves

1. Preheat oven to 425°. Position oven rack in next to lowest setting. Place a 16-inch pizza pan on the rack.

2. Heat a large nonstick skillet over medium-high heat. Add olive oil to pan; swirl to coat. Add onion and thyme to pan; cook 3 minutes or until onion is tender, stirring occasionally. Add bell pepper and garlic to pan; cook 2 minutes, stirring occasionally. Add corn, black pepper, and salt to pan; cook 1 minute or until mixture is thoroughly heated.

3. Roll dough into a 16-inch circle on a lightly floured surface. Remove pan from oven. Coat pan with cooking spray. Place dough on pan. Arrange mozzarella slices evenly over dough. Spread corn mixture evenly over cheese, and top with Parmigiano-Reggiano cheese. Bake at 425° for 23 minutes. Arrange tomatoes evenly over pizza; bake 5 more minutes or until crust is golden. Remove from oven; sprinkle with basil.

ROASTED BEET PIZZA

makes: 8 servings   hands-on time: 9 min.   total time: 1 hour, 27 min.

If you know someone who doesn't like beets, this pizza might convert them. Roast several golden beets at once, and enjoy the extras with salads, on sandwiches, or as a snack with crusty bread and goat cheese.

1   (4-oz.) golden beet

Yellow cornmeal

1   lb. prepared pizza dough, at room temperature

2   tsp. olive oil

½   cup (2 oz.) crumbled feta cheese

¼   cup vertically sliced shallots

¼   tsp. kosher salt

1   tsp. honey

1. Preheat oven to 450°.

2. Leave root and 1 inch of stem on beet; scrub with a brush. Wrap beet in foil. Bake at 450° for 40 minutes or until tender. Remove from oven; cool. Trim off beet root; rub off skin. Cut beet in half crosswise; thinly slice halves.

3. Position oven rack in lowest setting. Place a pizza stone or heavy baking sheet on the rack.

4. Increase oven temperature to 500° (keep pizza stone or baking sheet in oven as it preheats). Preheat pizza stone or baking sheet 30 minutes before baking pizza.

5. Sprinkle cornmeal on a baking sheet without raised edges. Roll dough into a 10-inch circle on prepared pan. Gently brush oil over dough. Arrange cheese, beet slices, and shallots evenly over dough, leaving a ½-inch border. Slide dough onto preheated pizza stone or heavy baking sheet, using a spatula as a guide.

6. Bake at 500° for 8 minutes or until crust is golden. Remove from pizza stone. Sprinkle with salt, and drizzle with honey.

HERBED TOMATO TART

makes: 6 servings hands-on time: 25 min. total time: 1 hour, 10 min.

2   medium tomatoes, thinly sliced (about ¾ lb.)

½   pt. assorted small tomatoes, halved

¾   tsp. salt, divided

1   (17.3-oz.) package frozen puff pastry sheets, thawed

1   (8-oz.) package shredded mozzarella cheese

1   (4-oz.) package crumbled feta cheese

¼   cup finely chopped chives

1   garlic clove, minced

¼   cup finely chopped assorted fresh herbs

1   Tbsp. olive oil

1. Preheat oven to 400°. Place tomatoes in a single layer on paper towels; sprinkle with ½ tsp. salt. Let stand 30 minutes. Pat dry with paper towels.

2. Meanwhile, roll 1 pastry sheet into a 14-inch square on a lightly floured surface; place on an ungreased baking sheet. Cut 4 (12- x 1-inch) strips from remaining pastry sheet, and place strips along outer edges of pastry square, forming a border. Reserve remaining pastry sheet for another use.

3. Bake at 400° for 14 minutes or until browned.

4. Sprinkle pastry with mozzarella cheese and next 3 ingredients. Top with tomatoes in a single layer. Sprinkle tomatoes with herbs and remaining ¼ tsp. salt; drizzle with oil.

5. Bake at 400° for 14 to 15 minutes or until cheese melts. Serve immediately.

PIZZA POINTER

We used basil, dill, thyme, and parsley, but just about any combination of herbs that pairs well with tomatoes—such as oregano and tarragon—would also work.

GRILLED TOMATO-PEACH PIZZA

makes: 6 servings hands-on time: 33 min. total time: 48 min.

Vegetable cooking spray

2   tomatoes, sliced

½   tsp. salt

1   large peach, peeled and sliced

1   lb. prepared pizza dough, at room temperature

½   (16-oz.) package fresh mozzarella cheese, sliced

4   to 6 fresh basil leaves

Garnishes: coarsely ground pepper, olive oil

1. Coat cold cooking grate of grill with cooking spray, and place on grill. Preheat grill to 300° to 350° (medium) heat.

2. Sprinkle tomatoes with salt; let stand 15 minutes. Pat tomatoes dry with paper towels.

3. Grill peach slices, covered with grill lid, 2 to 3 minutes on each side or until grill marks appear.

4. Place dough on a large baking sheet coated with cooking spray; lightly coat dough with cooking spray. Roll dough to ¼-inch thickness (about 14 inches in diameter). Slide pizza dough from baking sheet onto cooking grate.

5. Grill, covered with grill lid, 2 to 3 minutes or until lightly browned. Turn dough over, and reduce temperature to 250° to 300° (low) heat; top with tomatoes, grilled peaches, and mozzarella. Grill, covered with grill lid, 5 more minutes or until cheese melts. Arrange basil leaves over pizza. Serve immediately.

serve with
NUTTY GREEN BEANS

makes: 4 servings
hands-on time: 5 min.
total time: 10 min.

1   (12-oz.) package frozen steam-in-bag whole green beans

1   Tbsp. butter

1   Tbsp. lemon zest

1   Tbsp. lemon juice

3   Tbsp. roasted pecan-and-almond pieces

1. Cook green beans according to package directions.

2. Toss green beans with butter, lemon zest, and lemon juice.

3. Sprinkle with nut mixture; add salt and pepper to taste.

PORTOBELLO PIZZA

makes: 6 servings hands-on time: 15 min. total time: 38 min.

2   large portobello mushroom caps, sliced*

½   large onion, sliced

½   tsp. salt

½   tsp. pepper

Vegetable cooking spray

1   Tbsp. balsamic vinegar

Yellow cornmeal

1   (13.8-oz.) can refrigerated pizza dough

2   Tbsp. jarred pesto sauce

2   Tbsp. plain nonfat yogurt

¼   cup chopped fresh basil

6   fresh mozzarella cheese slices (6 oz.)**

5   plum tomatoes, chopped

2   Tbsp. shredded Parmesan cheese

1. Preheat oven to 425°. Sauté first 4 ingredients in a large skillet coated with cooking spray over medium-high heat 5 minutes or until onion is tender. Add balsamic vinegar; cook 2 minutes or until liquid is evaporated. Set aside.

2. Sprinkle cornmeal over baking pan; spread out pizza dough. Bake at 425° on bottom oven rack 5 minutes.

3. Stir together pesto and yogurt. Spread over pizza crust, leaving a 1-inch border. Sprinkle pizza with mushroom mixture and fresh basil. Top with mozzarella cheese and tomatoes. Sprinkle with Parmesan cheese.

4. Bake at 425° on bottom oven rack 18 more minutes or until edges are golden brown and cheese is melted.

* 1 (8-oz.) package sliced button mushrooms may be substituted for the portobello mushroom caps.

** 1½ cups (6 oz.) shredded part-skim mozzarella cheese may be substituted for fresh mozzarella.

Pizza Pointer

Let a cremini mushroom grow a few days longer, and you end up with a portobello. This flying saucer–shaped mushroom, which often measures from 3 to 6 inches across, is firm, meaty, and intensely flavorful.

SWEET POTATO-BRIE PIZZA

makes: 4 to 6 servings hands-on time: 8 min. total time: 38 min.

Use the herbs you have on hand; we recommend 1 Tbsp. chopped rosemary as a substitute for the sage.

3   Tbsp. garlic-flavored olive oil, divided

1   lb. prepared whole wheat pizza dough, at room temperature

1   medium-size sweet potato (about 8 oz.), peeled

1   Fuji apple, thinly sliced

2   shallots, sliced

¼   tsp. freshly ground pepper

¼   cup firmly packed brown sugar

1   (8-oz.) Brie round, cut into ½-inch cubes

10 small fresh sage leaves

1. Preheat oven to 450°. Brush a 15- x 10-inch jelly-roll pan with 1 Tbsp. olive oil. Stretch dough into a 15- x 10-inch rectangle on pan. Brush 1 Tbsp. olive oil on dough.

2. Thinly slice sweet potato crosswise. Toss sweet potato, apple, shallots, and remaining 1 Tbsp. olive oil in a bowl. Arrange sweet potato, apple, and shallots over dough. Sprinkle with pepper.

3. Bake at 450° for 20 minutes or until edges are golden and potatoes and apples are slightly cooked. Remove from oven; sprinkle with brown sugar, and top with cheese. Bake 10 more minutes or until cheese is melted. Sprinkle with sage leaves.

serve with
SAUTÉED ZUCCHINI SPEARS

makes: 4 servings
hands-on time: 8 min.
total time: 13 min.

3   medium zucchini

1½ tsp. olive oil

½   cup coarsely chopped onion

1. Cut zucchini in half lengthwise; cut each half crosswise into 2 pieces. Cut each piece into 3 spears.

2. Heat olive oil in a large nonstick skillet over medium-high heat; add zucchini and onion. Sauté 5 to 6 minutes or until vegetables are lightly browned. Sprinkle with salt and pepper to taste; toss well.

PEAR, HAZELNUT & GOUDA PIZZAS

makes: 6 servings   hands-on time: 15 min.   total time: 21 min.

If you're short on time, buy a favorite bottled vinaigrette to toss with the salad greens.

Vegetable cooking spray

1½ lb. prepared whole wheat pizza dough, at room temperature

Parchment paper

¼ cup hazelnut oil or olive oil, divided

1½ cups shredded smoked Gouda cheese

2 ripe Bosc pears, thinly sliced

1 Tbsp. balsamic vinegar

1 Tbsp. finely chopped shallot

1½ tsp. honey

⅛ tsp. salt

⅛ tsp. freshly ground pepper

3 cups loosely packed gourmet mixed salad greens

⅔ cup toasted hazelnuts, coarsely chopped

1. Coat cold cooking grate of grill with cooking spray, and place on grill. Preheat grill to 300° to 350° (medium) heat.

2. Divide pizza dough into 6 equal portions. Roll 1 portion of dough at a time into a 6-inch round on a lightly floured surface. Transfer dough rounds to a parchment paper-lined baking sheet. Brush dough with 1 Tbsp. hazelnut oil.

3. Slide pizza dough rounds off baking sheet; flip dough over onto cooking grate of grill. Grill, covered with grill lid, 2 minutes. Brush tops with 1 Tbsp. hazelnut oil. Flip pizzas, and top evenly with cheese and pear slices. Grill 3 more minutes or until crusts are golden brown and cheese is melted.

4. Whisk together vinegar, next 4 ingredients, and remaining 2 Tbsp. hazelnut oil in a bowl. Add salad greens; toss to coat. Top each pizza with about ½ cup salad greens. Sprinkle with hazelnuts.

Pizza Pointer

Work quickly to top each pizza with cheese and pear slices while pizzas are on the grill. We recommend using spring-loaded tongs.

SALAD ON A PIZZA!

HARVEST PIZZA

makes: 4 to 6 servings   hands-on time: 10 min.   total time: 28 min.

1　lb. prepared pizza dough, at room temperature

Yellow cornmeal

1　cup mashed sweet potatoes or leftover sweet potato casserole (without toppings)

1　cup shredded roasted turkey

1　cup shredded spinach

½　cup sliced shiitake mushrooms

½　cup sliced red onion

1½　cups (6 oz.) shredded Havarti cheese

1　tsp. freshly ground Italian seasoning

1. Preheat oven to 450°. Roll dough into a 12-inch circle. Transfer to a baking sheet sprinkled with cornmeal.

2. Spread mashed sweet potatoes over dough. Top with turkey, spinach, mushrooms, sliced red onion, cheese, and Italian seasoning.

3. Bake at 450° directly on oven rack 18 minutes or until edges are browned.

This pizza is quick to make because it uses prepared ingredients like pizza dough, cooked turkey, and leftover mashed sweet potatoes.

SPEED It Up!

APPLE-GOAT CHEESE PIZZA

makes: 6 servings hands-on time: 20 min. total time: 40 min.

Tart apple slices, sweet figs, and creamy goat cheese combine in a fun, fresh spin on pizza. Cut into smaller pieces for a great appetizer.

1   **(11-oz.) can refrigerated thin pizza crust dough**

1   **Granny Smith apple, thinly sliced**

½   **cup thinly sliced red onion**

2   **tsp. olive oil**

⅓   **cup fig preserves**

4   **oz. crumbled goat cheese**

1   **cup arugula**

½   **cup chopped toasted pecans**

1. Preheat oven to 450°. Unroll dough; pat to an even thickness on a lightly greased baking sheet. Bake at 450° for 10 to 12 minutes or until lightly browned.

2. Sauté apple and onion in hot olive oil in a nonstick skillet until tender. Spread fig preserves over crust. Top with apple mixture and goat cheese. Bake at 450° for 8 to 10 minutes or until cheese is slightly melted. Top with arugula and pecans.

GRAPE, BLUE CHEESE & WALNUT PIZZA

makes: 2 servings hands-on time: 4 min. total time: 14 min.

Whole-wheat flatbread makes this thin and crunchy crust super simple.

1 **(2.8-oz.) whole wheat flatbread**

¾ **cup seedless red grapes, halved**

2 **Tbsp. crumbled blue cheese**

2 **Tbsp. chopped walnuts, toasted**

2 **Tbsp. balsamic vinegar**

1 **cup arugula leaves**

1. Preheat oven to 375°.

2. Place flatbread on rack in oven; bake at 375° for 3 minutes or until lightly browned. Remove flatbread from oven; top with grapes, cheese, and walnuts. Return flatbread to oven; bake 5 minutes or until cheese melts and crust is browned.

3. While pizza bakes, bring vinegar to a boil in a small saucepan. Boil 1 minute or until vinegar thickens and reduces to about ½ Tbsp. Top pizza with arugula; drizzle with balsamic syrup. Serve immediately.

Note: We tested with Flatout Harvest Wheat flatbread.

You can substitute bottled balsamic glaze instead of taking the time to reduce your own.

SPEED IT UP!

HOT OFF THE GRILL!

GRILLED PIZZA
WITH ASPARAGUS & CARAMELIZED ONION

makes: 2 servings hands-on time: 38 min. total time: 38 min.

1 Tbsp. extra virgin olive oil, divided

2 cups thinly vertically sliced onion

2 cups (2-inch) sliced asparagus (about ½ lb.)

1 Tbsp. thinly sliced ready-to-use sun-dried tomatoes

⅛ tsp. salt

1 lb. prepared pizza dough, at room temperature

¾ cup (3 oz.) shredded fontina cheese

1½ tsp. fresh oregano leaves

¼ tsp. freshly ground black pepper

1. Preheat grill to 350° to 400° (medium-high) heat.

2. Heat 2 tsp. oil in a large nonstick skillet over medium-high heat. Add onion to pan; sauté 5 minutes. Reduce heat to medium-low; cook 5 minutes or until browned. Add asparagus to pan; cook 5 minutes or until asparagus is crisp-tender. Stir in tomatoes and salt.

3. Roll dough into a 12-inch circle on a lightly floured surface; brush each side of dough with ½ tsp. oil.

4. Place dough on grill rack; grill 1½ minutes or until crust bubbles and is well marked. Reduce grill heat to low; turn dough over. Arrange onion mixture over crust; sprinkle evenly with cheese. Grill, covered with grill lid, over low heat 3½ minutes or until cheese melts; remove pizza from grill. Sprinkle with oregano and black pepper.

serve with
SESAME-GINGER CUCUMBERS

makes: 2 cups
hands-on time: 5 min.
total time: 5 min.

1 English cucumber, thinly sliced into half moons

3 Tbsp. sesame-ginger vinaigrette

1 Tbsp. chopped fresh cilantro

1 tsp. toasted sesame seeds

1. Stir together all ingredients. Cover and chill until ready to serve.

ROASTED GARLIC PIZZA

makes: 4 servings   hands-on time: 12 min.   total time: 2 hours, 17 min.

A slice of this pizza makes a tasty appetizer, or serve two slices with a tossed salad for supper.

1   **whole garlic bulb**

1   **lb. prepared pizza dough, at room temperature**

Yellow cornmeal

1   **cup (4 oz.) shredded part-skim mozzarella cheese**

¼   **cup (1 oz.) grated Parmigiano-Reggiano cheese**

2   **tsp. chopped fresh oregano**

¼   **tsp. dried crushed red pepper**

1. Preheat oven to 375°.

2. Remove white papery skin from garlic bulb (do not peel or separate the cloves). Wrap garlic in foil. Bake at 375° for 45 minutes; cool 10 minutes. Separate cloves; squeeze to extract garlic pulp. Discard skins.

3. Increase oven temperature to 400°.

4. Roll dough into a 10-inch circle on a lightly floured surface. Place dough on pizza pan or baking sheet sprinkled with cornmeal. Spread roasted garlic evenly over pizza, leaving a ½-inch border; top with cheeses, oregano, and pepper. Bake at 400° for 12 minutes or until crust is golden.

If you're short on time, skip roasting your own garlic and substitute jarred roasted garlic.

Speed It Up!

MINI PESTO PIZZAS
WITH ZUCCHINI RIBBONS, FONTINA & EGGS

makes: 4 servings   hands-on time: 15 min.   total time: 37 min., including pesto

Make an indentation in the melted cheese with the back of a spoon to create a "nest" for the egg.

1   lb. prepared pizza dough, at room temperature

2   Tbsp. olive oil

Basil-Mint Pesto

1   cup (4 oz.) shredded fontina cheese

1   medium zucchini, halved lengthwise

4   large eggs

Fresh basil leaves

1. Preheat oven to 500°. Divide dough into 4 equal portions. Shape each portion into a 4-inch round on a lightly greased baking sheet. Brush dough rounds with olive oil. Spread rounds evenly with Basil-Mint Pesto; sprinkle with cheese.

2. Cut zucchini lengthwise into thin ribbons using a vegetable peeler. Arrange zucchini evenly on pizzas. Make a well in center of each pizza.

3. Bake at 500° for 7 minutes or just until edges begin to brown. Gently break 1 egg onto center of each pizza. Bake 7 more minutes or to desired degree of doneness. Just before serving, season with salt and pepper to taste; top with basil.

BASIL-MINT PESTO

makes: about ¾ cup
hands-on time: 8 min.
total time: 8 min.

1½   cups loosely packed fresh basil leaves

½   cup loosely packed fresh mint leaves

⅓   cup grated Asiago or Parmesan cheese

¼   cup extra virgin olive oil

¼   cup pine nuts, toasted

1   tsp. lemon juice

¼   tsp. salt

¼   tsp. freshly ground pepper

¼   tsp. dried crushed red pepper

3   garlic cloves

1. Process all ingredients in a food processor until smooth, stopping to scrape down sides as needed.

SHRIMP-PESTO PIZZAS

makes: 6 servings hands-on time: 37 min. total time: 47 min.

Vegetable cooking spray

1 lb. unpeeled, large raw shrimp

1 large yellow onion, chopped

1 red bell pepper, chopped

¼ tsp. salt

¼ tsp. pepper

1½ tsp. olive oil

1½ lb. prepared pizza dough, at room temperature

All-purpose flour

Yellow cornmeal

½ cup Basil Pesto (page 12)

¾ cup freshly grated Parmesan cheese

Take some shortcuts by buying prechopped onion and bell peppers and substituting prepared pesto.

Speed It Up!

1. Coat cold cooking grate of grill with cooking spray, and place on grill. Preheat grill to 300° to 350° (medium) heat.

2. Peel shrimp, and slice in half lengthwise; devein, if desired.

3. Sauté onion, bell pepper, salt, and pepper in ½ tsp. hot oil in a large skillet over medium heat 5 minutes or until tender. Transfer onion mixture to a large bowl. Sauté shrimp in remaining 1 tsp. hot oil 3 minutes or just until shrimp turn pink. Add shrimp to onion mixture, and toss.

4. Divide dough into 6 equal portions. Lightly sprinkle flour on a large surface. Roll each portion into a 6-inch round (about ¼ inch thick). Carefully transfer pizza dough rounds to a cutting board or baking sheet sprinkled with cornmeal.

5. Slide pizza dough rounds onto cooking grate of grill; spread Basil Pesto over rounds, and top with shrimp mixture. Sprinkle each with 2 Tbsp. Parmesan cheese.

6. Grill, covered with grill lid, 4 minutes. Rotate pizzas one-quarter turn, and grill, covered with grill lid, 5 to 6 more minutes or until pizza crusts are cooked. Serve immediately.

ARTICHOKE PIZZA
WITH ARUGULA & PROSCIUTTO

makes: 6 servings   hands-on time: 13 min.   total time: 24 min.

With artichokes, arugula, pesto, prosciutto, and Parmesan, this pizza has intense flavor. Splurge and try it with Basil Pesto (page 12) when you can get fresh basil.

Vegetable cooking spray

Yellow cornmeal

1   (13.8-oz.) can refrigerated pizza crust dough

2   Tbsp. jarred pesto sauce

¾   cup (3 oz.) shredded part-skim mozzarella cheese

1   (9-oz.) package frozen artichoke hearts, thawed and drained

1   oz. thinly sliced prosciutto

2   Tbsp. shredded Parmesan cheese

1½   cups arugula

1½   Tbsp. fresh lemon juice

1. Position oven rack in lowest setting. Preheat oven to 500°.

2. Coat a baking sheet with cooking spray; sprinkle with cornmeal. Unroll dough onto prepared baking sheet, and pat into a 14- x 10-inch rectangle. Spread pesto evenly over dough, leaving a ½-inch border. Sprinkle mozzarella cheese over pesto. Place baking sheet on bottom rack in oven; bake at 500° for 5 minutes. Remove pizza from oven.

3. Coarsely chop artichokes. Arrange artichokes on pizza; top with sliced prosciutto. Sprinkle with Parmesan. Return pizza to bottom rack in oven; bake 6 more minutes or until crust is golden.

4. Place arugula in a bowl. Drizzle lemon juice over arugula; toss gently. Top pizza with arugula mixture. Cut pizza into 6 (5- x 4-inch) rectangles; cut each rectangle diagonally into 2 wedges.

PROSCIUTTO PIZZA
WITH TANGY WHITE SAUCE

makes: 6 servings   hands-on time: 15 min.   total time: 53 min.

A homemade white sauce makes all the difference with this simple pizza. Top it with salty prosciutto just before serving.

Yellow cornmeal

1   **lb. prepared pizza dough, at room temperature**

1½   **tsp. olive oil**

¾   **cup 2% reduced-fat milk**

2   **tsp. Dijon mustard**

½   **tsp. freshly ground black pepper**

1   **large egg yolk**

1½   **Tbsp. butter**

1½   **tsp. minced fresh garlic**

2   **tsp. all-purpose flour**

¾   **cup (3 oz.) shredded Gruyère cheese**

2   **oz. thinly sliced prosciutto, torn**

1   **Tbsp. chopped fresh chives**

1. Sprinkle cornmeal on a lightly floured baking sheet without raised edges. Roll dough into a 13-inch circle on prepared baking sheet. Brush dough evenly with 1½ tsp. olive oil. Cover dough loosely with plastic wrap.

2. Place a pizza stone or heavy baking sheet in oven. Preheat oven to 500° (keep pizza stone or baking sheet in oven as it preheats). Preheat pizza stone or baking sheet 30 minutes before baking pizza.

3. Combine milk and next 3 ingredients in a medium bowl, stirring with a whisk. Melt butter in a medium saucepan over low heat. Add garlic; cook 3 minutes or just until butter and garlic begin to brown, stirring frequently. Add flour to pan; cook 30 seconds, stirring constantly with a whisk. Stir in milk mixture; bring to a boil. Cook 1 minute or until thick, stirring constantly. Remove plastic wrap from dough.

4. Spread sauce over dough; sprinkle evenly with cheese. Slide pizza onto preheated pizza stone or heavy baking sheet, using a spatula as a guide.

5. Bake at 500° for 18 minutes or until crust is golden. Arrange prosciutto on pizza; sprinkle with chives. Cut pizza into 12 wedges.

HAM & CHEESE MAKEOVER

GORGONZOLA PIZZA
WITH DATES, PROSCIUTTO & ALMONDS

makes: 4 to 6 servings hands-on time: 12 min. total time: 45 min.

Wow your crowd with this decadent white pizza featuring caramelized shallots and sweet Medjool dates.

- 1 **lb. prepared whole wheat pizza dough, at room temperature**
- **Yellow cornmeal**
- 1 **cup sliced shallots (4 large)**
- 1 **Tbsp. olive oil, divided**
- 2 **tsp. sherry vinegar**
- ⅓ **cup refrigerated Alfredo sauce**
- ⅔ **cup crumbled Gorgonzola cheese**
- ½ **cup chopped dried Medjool dates**
- 2 **oz. thinly sliced prosciutto, cut crosswise into ½-inch pieces**
- ½ **tsp. fresh rosemary leaves**
- ⅓ **cup whole Marcona almonds, toasted**

1. Preheat oven to 450°. Heat pizza stone according to manufacturer's instructions. Roll dough into a 12-inch circle on a lightly floured surface. Sprinkle cornmeal on preheated stone; place dough on stone. Bake at 450° for 13 minutes.

2. Sauté shallots in hot oil in a non-stick skillet over medium heat 10 minutes or until tender. Add vinegar, and cook 2 more minutes or until vinegar is absorbed.

3. Spread Alfredo sauce evenly on pizza dough, leaving a ½-inch border. Top with sautéed shallots, Gorgonzola cheese, dates, and prosciutto. Sprinkle with rosemary.

4. Bake at 450° for 15 minutes or until crust is golden and cheese is bubbly. Sprinkle with toasted almonds. Let stand 5 minutes before serving.

BACON, TOMATO & ARUGULA PIZZA

makes: 4 to 6 servings   hands-on time: 17 min.   total time: 35 min.

5 slices applewood-smoked bacon

2 cups grape tomatoes, halved lengthwise

½ tsp. dried crushed red pepper

Yellow cornmeal

1 lb. prepared whole wheat pizza dough, at room temperature

½ cup lower-sodium marinara sauce

¾ cup (3 oz.) shredded part-skim mozzarella cheese

1 cup arugula

1 tsp. extra virgin olive oil

½ tsp. white wine vinegar

1. Position oven rack in lowest setting. Preheat oven to 450°.

2. Cook bacon in a large nonstick skillet over medium heat until crisp. Remove bacon from pan, reserving 2 tsp. drippings; crumble bacon, and set aside. Add tomatoes and red pepper to drippings in pan; cook 2 minutes, stirring occasionally.

3. Sprinkle a large baking sheet with cornmeal; roll dough into a 12-inch circle on prepared baking sheet. Spread sauce over dough; top with tomato mixture. Sprinkle bacon and cheese over tomato mixture.

4. Bake at 450° on bottom rack in oven 17 minutes or until crust is golden. Combine arugula, oil, and vinegar; top pizza with arugula mixture.

serve with

HONEYED CARROTS

makes: 2 cups
hands-on time: 2 min.
total time: 12 min.

1 (16-oz.) package baby carrots

2 Tbsp. honey

1 Tbsp. butter

2 tsp. lemon juice

¼ tsp. salt

1. Combine all ingredients in a medium-size microwave-safe dish. Cover and microwave at HIGH 8 to 10 minutes or until tender, stirring after 4 minutes.

THE FARMER'S PIZZA

makes: 4 to 6 servings hands-on time: 10 min. total time: 50 min.

2   **oz. thinly sliced pancetta**

1   **cup thinly sliced sweet onion**

1   **lb. prepared pizza dough, at room temperature**

1   **Tbsp. olive oil**

1   **cup Spicy Tomato Pizza Sauce (page 10)**

1   **cup cherry tomatoes, halved**

½   **cup mascarpone cheese, softened and divided**

2   **cups packed arugula leaves**

Pizza Pointer

Dollops of mascarpone cheese melt into this pizza as it bakes, balancing out the spice of the sauce.

1. Place a pizza stone or baking sheet in oven. Preheat oven to 450° for 30 minutes. Cook pancetta in a large skillet over medium-high heat 3 minutes or until cooked but not crisp, turning often. Drain on paper towels, reserving drippings in skillet. Cook onion in hot drippings, stirring often, 5 minutes or until tender.

2. Stretch pizza dough into a 12-inch circle on a lightly floured surface. (No need to perfect the round shape.) Place on a lightly floured baking sheet. Brush olive oil over dough using a pastry brush. (If you don't have a pastry brush, drizzle oil evenly over dough.) Cover loosely with plastic wrap, and let rise in a warm place (85°), free from drafts, 20 to 25 minutes.

3. Remove and discard plastic wrap from dough. Slide dough from baking sheet onto hot pizza stone or baking sheet in oven. Bake at 450° for 5 minutes.

4. Spread pizza sauce over partially baked crust, leaving a 1-inch border. Top with tomatoes, pancetta, and onion. Dollop ¼ cup cheese by rounded tablespoonfuls over pizza.

5. Bake at 450° for 15 minutes or until crust is golden. Immediately dollop remaining ¼ cups cheese over pizza. Sprinkle with arugula.

READY IN 15 MINUTES!

GREEK PIZZA
WITH CHICKEN & ARTICHOKES

makes: 4 servings   hands-on time: 10 min.   total time: 15 min.

1 lb. prepared pizza dough, at room temperature

1½ cups (6 oz.) shredded mozzarella cheese, divided

2 cups shredded rotisserie chicken

1 (7-oz.) jar roasted red bell peppers, drained and cut into strips

1 (6-oz.) jar marinated artichoke hearts, drained and coarsely chopped

10 kalamata olives, drained, pitted, and thinly sliced

1½ Tbsp. chopped fresh oregano

1 Tbsp. olive oil

½ tsp. freshly ground pepper

1 cup crumbled feta cheese

1. Preheat oven to 500°.

2. On a lightly floured surface, roll out pizza dough into a 15-inch circle. Sprinkle ¾ cup mozzarella cheese onto prepared pizza dough. Top evenly with chicken.

3. Combine roasted red bell peppers and next 5 ingredients in a bowl; toss gently. Spoon mixture evenly over chicken. Sprinkle with remaining ¾ cup mozzarella cheese; top with feta cheese.

4. Bake at 500° for 5 to 7 minutes or until browned and bubbly.

Pizza Pointer

It's easiest to shred rotisserie chicken while the chicken's still warm; if it's cold, just warm it in the oven at 350° for 15 minutes.

SOUTHWESTERN PIZZA

makes: 4 servings   hands-on time: 10 min.   total time: 20 min.

Two tortillas sandwiched with cheese make these individual pizzas extra sturdy and super tasty.

8   **(10-inch) flour tortillas**

1   **(8-oz.) package shredded Mexican four-cheese blend**

1   **cup chunky salsa**

Black Bean Salsa

2   **cups chopped cooked chicken**

1. Preheat oven to 400°. Place 4 flour tortillas on a lightly greased baking sheet. Top tortillas evenly with 1 cup cheese; cover with remaining flour tortillas.

2. Divide chunky salsa, Black Bean Salsa, chicken, and remaining 1 cup cheese over flour tortillas. Bake at 400° for 10 minutes or until cheese is bubbly. Cut into wedges.

BLACK BEAN SALSA

makes: 3 cups
hands-on time: 10 min.
total time: 10 min.

1   **(15-oz.) can black beans, drained and rinsed**

½   **cup frozen whole kernel corn, thawed**

2   **plum tomatoes, seeded and chopped**

1   **green onion, chopped**

2   **Tbsp. fresh lime juice**

1   **Tbsp. chopped fresh cilantro**

1   **garlic clove, pressed**

½   **tsp. Creole seasoning**

1. Stir together all ingredients. Cover and chill until ready to serve.

THIS PIZZA STACKS UP!

TURKEY CLUB PIZZA

makes: 4 to 6 servings hands-on time: 20 min. total time: 40 min.

1 (11-oz.) can refrigerated thin pizza crust dough

¼ cup mayonnaise

3 Tbsp. jarred pesto sauce

2 cups cubed cooked turkey

2 thinly sliced plum tomatoes

¼ cup thinly sliced red onion

1½ cups (6 oz.) shredded colby-Jack cheese

4 cooked and crumbled bacon slices

Chopped fresh avocado

1. Preheat oven to 450°. Unroll dough; pat to an even thickness on a lightly greased baking sheet. Bake at 450° for 10 to 12 minutes or until lightly browned.

2. Stir together mayonnaise and pesto sauce; spread over crust. Top with turkey, tomatoes, and onion. Bake at 450° for 6 to 8 minutes. Sprinkle with cheese and bacon. Bake until cheese melts. Top with avocado.

Pizza Pointer

Use leftover turkey in this fun twist on a club sandwich, or look for rotisserie turkey in your local market.

MUFFULETTA CALZONES

makes: 4 servings hands-on time: 20 min. total time: 40 min.

Pizza dough from the grocery store bakery encases traditional muffuletta ingredients— salami, ham, cheese, and olives.

1   cup jarred mixed pickled vegetables, rinsed and finely chopped

1   (7-oz.) package shredded provolone-Italian cheese blend

8   thin slices Genoa salami, chopped (about ⅛ lb.)

½   cup diced cooked ham

¼   cup sliced pimiento-stuffed Spanish olives

2   Tbsp. olive oil, divided

1   lb. prepared pizza dough, at room temperature

2   Tbsp. grated Parmesan cheese

Little Helpers

Let kids help assemble calzones by filling crusts and sealing edges. Then they can brush tops with oil and sprinkle with cheese.

1. Preheat oven to 425°. Stir together pickled vegetables, next 4 ingredients, and 1 Tbsp. olive oil.

2. Place dough on a lightly floured surface. Cut dough into 4 equal pieces. Roll each piece into a 7-inch circle.

3. Place 2 dough circles on a lightly greased baking sheet. Spoon vegetable mixture on top of dough circles, mounding mixture on dough and leaving a 1-inch border. Moisten edges of dough with water, and top with remaining 2 dough circles. Press and crimp edges to seal.

4. Cut small slits in tops of dough to allow steam to escape. Brush with remaining 1 Tbsp. olive oil, and sprinkle with Parmesan cheese.

5. Bake at 425° for 20 to 24 minutes or until golden brown.

BARBECUED PORK & PINEAPPLE PIZZA

makes: 6 to 8 servings   hands-on time: 25 min.   total time: 1 hour, 43 min.

Slow-cooked pork gives this Hawaiian-style pizza rich flavor.

- 2   Tbsp. olive oil, divided
- 1½ lb. prepared whole wheat pizza dough, at room temperature
- 1   large red onion, thinly sliced and separated into rings
- ½   cup barbecue sauce
- 1   cup shredded barbecued pork
- ½   cup chopped fresh pineapple
- 1   cup shredded smoked Gouda cheese
- 1   cup (4 oz.) shredded fontina cheese
- ¼   cup chopped fresh cilantro

1. Preheat oven to 450°. Brush a jelly-roll pan with 1 Tbsp. olive oil. Stretch dough into a 14-inch circle on pan.

2. Sauté onion in remaining 1 Tbsp. hot oil in a large non-stick skillet over medium-high heat 10 to 15 minutes or until tender.

3. Spread barbecue sauce on pizza dough, leaving a ½-inch border. Top with shredded pork, pineapple, and sautéed onion. Sprinkle with cheeses.

4. Bake at 450° for 18 to 20 minutes or until crust is golden. Sprinkle with cilantro.

serve with
ONION-AND-HERB COLESLAW

makes: 5 cups
hands-on time: 5 min.
total time: 5 min.

- ⅓   cup mayonnaise
- ¼   cup buttermilk
- 1   tsp. salt-free onion-and-herb seasoning blend
- ¼   tsp. salt
- ⅛   tsp. pepper
- 1   (16-oz.) package shredded coleslaw mix

1. Whisk together first 5 ingredients until well blended. Pour mayonnaise mixture over shredded coleslaw mix; toss well. Chill until ready to serve.

GRILLED PIZZA
WITH STEAK, PEAR & ARUGULA

makes: 4 servings   hands-on time: 40 min.   total time: 50 min.

Vegetable cooking spray

½   lb. flank steak

Salt and pepper

1   Tbsp. olive oil

1½ tsp. white balsamic vinegar

1   (12-inch) prebaked pizza crust

1   red Bartlett pear, peeled and sliced

1½ cups fresh arugula, divided

¼   cup crumbled Gorgonzola cheese

Freshly cracked pepper

1. Coat cold cooking grate of grill with cooking spray, and place on grill. Preheat grill to 300° to 350° (medium) heat.

2. Season flank steak with desired amount of salt and pepper.

3. Grill steak, covered with grill lid, 8 to 10 minutes on each side or to desired degree of doneness. Cover and let stand 10 minutes.

4. Meanwhile, whisk together oil and vinegar in a small bowl.

5. Cut steak diagonally across grain into thin strips. Cut strips into bite-size pieces (about 1 cup).

6. Place pizza crust directly on hot cooking grate. Brush top of crust with oil mixture; layer with pear slices, 1 cup arugula, cheese, and beef strips.

7. Grill, covered with grill lid, 4 minutes. Rotate pizza one-quarter turn; grill, covered with grill lid, 5 to 6 more minutes or until thoroughly heated. Remove pizza from grill, and sprinkle with remaining ½ cup arugula and freshly cracked pepper.

Oven-Baked Pizza with Steak, Pear & Arugula: Assemble pizza as directed, and bake according to package directions for pizza crust.

Use sliced leftover steak in place of the flank steak for an even quicker dinner.

SPEED It Up!

PROVENÇAL FLATBREAD

makes: 24 servings hands-on time: 30 min. total time: 30 min.

Herbes de Provence is a blend of herbs that thrive in the southeastern region of France—typically thyme, summer savory, fennel, basil, and lavender flowers.

Vegetable cooking spray

1   (13.8 oz.) can refrigerated pizza dough

3   Tbsp. extra virgin olive oil, divided

1   tsp. herbes de Provence

3   plum tomatoes, finely chopped (¾ cup)

½   cup chopped, pitted kalamata olives

4   garlic cloves, chopped

2   tsp. chopped fresh basil leaves

1   tsp. freshly ground pepper

½   tsp. coarse sea salt

Garnish: Fresh basil leaves or rosemary sprigs, if desired

1. Preheat oven to 400°. Spray a large baking sheet with cooking spray. Unroll dough on prepared baking sheet; starting at center, press out dough into a 15- x 10-inch rectangle. Brush with 1 Tbsp. oil; sprinkle with herbes de Provence.

2. Bake 15 to 18 minutes or until lightly browned.

3. Meanwhile, in a medium bowl, mix remaining 2 Tbsp. oil, tomatoes, and next 5 ingredients.

4. Cut flatbread into 24 pieces. Top evenly with tomato mixture. Garnish with basil leaves and rosemary, if desired.

PIZZA POINTER

Use the best extra virgin olive oil that you have—the fruity flavor of a good olive oil will shine in this recipe. You can also use garlic- or herb-infused oil.

CORNBREAD FOCACCIA

makes: 8 to 10 servings hands-on time: 15 min. total time: 45 min.

A sprinkling of yeast is stirred into the batter—but there's no rise time or kneading.

- 2 cups self-rising white cornmeal mix
- 2 cups buttermilk
- ½ cup all-purpose flour
- 1 (¼-oz.) envelope rapid-rise yeast
- 2 large eggs, lightly beaten
- ¼ cup butter, melted
- 2 Tbsp. sugar
- 1 cup crumbled feta cheese
- 1 cup coarsely chopped black olives
- ¾ cup grape tomatoes, cut in half
- 1 Tbsp. coarsely chopped fresh rosemary

1. Preheat oven to 375°. Heat a well-greased 12-inch cast-iron skillet in oven 5 minutes.

2. Stir together cornmeal mix and next 6 ingredients just until moistened; pour into hot skillet. Sprinkle with feta cheese, olives, tomatoes, and rosemary.

3. Bake at 375° for 30 minutes or until golden brown.

Self-rising cornmeal is a great time-saver because it includes several ingredients at once! If you don't have self-rising cornmeal, make your own by combining 1½ cups cornmeal, ⅓ cup all-purpose flour, 2 Tbsp. baking powder, and 1 tsp. salt.

SPEED IT UP!

PIZZA DOLCE

makes: 20 servings (2 pies) hands-on time: 10 min. total time: 9 hours, 10 min.

Serve this authentic Italian dessert to top off your pizza night. Sweet almond liqueur and decadent chocolate hit the spot after a savory pizza dinner.

2   (15-oz.) containers ricotta cheese

4   large eggs

1½ cups powdered sugar

1   Tbsp. lemon zest

3   Tbsp. fresh lemon juice

⅓   cup almond liqueur

1   cup semisweet choco-late mini-morsels

2   (9-inch) chocolate cookie crusts

1. Preheat oven to 350°. Stir together first 7 ingredients; pour evenly into crusts.

2. Bake at 350° for 35 to 40 minutes or until set and golden brown. Cool on wire racks. Chill 8 hours before serving.

APPLE-PINEAPPLE DESSERT PIZZA

makes: 8 servings hands-on time: 30 min. total time: 40 min.

1   (13.8-oz.) can refrigerated pizza crust dough

1   (15¼-oz.) can crushed pineapple

1   (20-oz.) can apple pie filling

1   tsp. cornstarch

¼   tsp. ground cinnamon

¼   tsp. ground nutmeg

1½ cups (6 oz.) shredded sharp Cheddar cheese

⅔   cup all-purpose flour

½   cup firmly packed brown sugar

¼   cup butter

⅓   cup finely chopped dried apricots

1. Preheat oven to 425°. Press dough into a lightly greased 11- x 7-inch baking dish. Bake at 425° for 7 minutes; cool. Increase oven temperature to 450°.

2. Drain pineapple, reserving ⅓ cup juice. Combine pineapple and pie filling. Stir together reserved pineapple juice, cornstarch, cinnamon, and nutmeg; add to pineapple mixture. Spoon evenly over crust; sprinkle with cheese.

3. Combine flour and brown sugar; cut in butter with a pastry blender until crumbly. Sprinkle crumble topping over cheese. Top evenly with dried apricots.

4. Bake at 450° for 10 to 12 minutes or until golden brown.

Little Helpers

Let kids press out pizza dough into the dish and make the crumble topping. When the hot filling is spread out over the pizza, kids can sprinkle with cheese, crumble topping, and apricots.

KIDS' FAVORITES

These simple, and sometimes silly, pizzas are sure to get the whole family excited for dinner.

PIZZA STICKS

makes: about 12 strips hands-on time: 6 min. total time: 18 min.

Jarred bruschetta topping, chock-full of flavorful herbs and veggies, saves both money and prep time for these cheesy pizza sticks. Simply top a refrigerated thin pizza crust with the bruschetta topping and a shredded cheese blend, bake, and cut into bite-size strips.

1 (10-oz.) thin pizza crust

1 (10.5-oz.) container tomato bruschetta topping

1 cup (4 oz.) shredded Italian cheese blend

Cut these pizza bites into fun shapes like triangles, circles, or stars to make them irresistible.

Little Helpers

1. Preheat oven to 450°. Top crust with tomato bruschetta topping. Sprinkle evenly with shredded Italian cheese blend. Bake at 450°, directly on oven rack, 12 minutes or until crust is golden and cheese is bubbly. Cut pizza in half, and cut each half lengthwise into 2-inch strips.

Note: We tested with Buitoni Classic Bruschetta topping.

STUFFED PIZZA ROLLS

makes: 16 appetizer servings   hands-on time: 15 min.   total time: 25 min.

2   (8-oz.) cans refrigerated crescent rolls

2   (6-oz.) packages pepperoni slices

4   (1-oz.) mozzarella cheese sticks, cut into fourths

2   tsp. dried Italian seasoning

½   tsp. garlic salt

1. Preheat oven to 375°. Separate each can of rolls into 8 triangles. Put 2 pepperoni slices on each triangle; place 1 piece cheese at wide end of triangle. Sprinkle with dried Italian seasoning. Roll up, starting at wide end. Place pizza rolls on an ungreased baking sheet. Sprinkle with garlic salt.

2. Bake at 375° for 10 to 12 minutes or until golden.

serve with

HOT FUDGE SUNDAE SHAKE

makes: 4 servings
hands-on time: 8 min.
total time: 8 min.

1   pt. vanilla bean ice cream

½   cup milk

8   Tbsp. hot fudge topping, warmed

8   Tbsp. caramel topping, warmed

1   (8.5-oz.) can refrigerated instant whipped cream

¼   cup crumbled brownies, divided

4   maraschino cherries (with stems)

1. Process ice cream and milk in a blender until smooth, stopping to scrape down sides.

2. Divide half of ice-cream mixture evenly among 4 (8-oz.) glasses. Top each with 1 Tbsp. fudge topping and 1 Tbsp. caramel topping. Repeat layers with remaining ice-cream mixture and fudge and caramel toppings.

3. Top each with instant whipped cream; sprinkle with 1 Tbsp. crumbled brownies, and top with a cherry. Serve immediately.

PIZZA MUFFINS

makes: 1 dozen   hands-on time: 15 min.   total time: 41 min.

Tomato juice lends these zesty muffins a tawny color. Serve them with a cup of soup or a salad for a satisfying lunch.

¼   cup finely chopped onion

1   garlic clove, minced

6   Tbsp. olive oil, divided

2   cups all-purpose flour

1   cup (4 oz.) shredded mozzarella cheese

¼   cup diced turkey pepperoni

2¾   tsp. baking powder

1   tsp. dried oregano

¾   tsp. salt

1   cup tomato juice

1   large egg

½   cup freshly grated Parmesan cheese

1. Preheat oven to 400°. Sauté onion and garlic in 2 Tbsp. hot oil in a large skillet over medium-high heat 2 to 3 minutes or until tender. Set aside.

2. Combine flour and next 5 ingredients in a large bowl; make a well in center of mixture.

3. Stir together onion mixture, tomato juice, egg, and remaining 4 Tbsp. oil, blending well; add to flour mixture, stirring just until dry ingredients are moistened. Spoon mixture into lightly greased muffin pans, filling two-thirds full. Sprinkle evenly with grated Parmesan cheese.

4. Bake at 400° for 20 minutes or until lightly browned. Let stand 3 minutes before removing from pans.

PIZZA POINTER

This is a great snack or dinner on-the-go! A couple of pizza muffins and a side of grapes will be the new Lunchbox favorite.

CHEESE-AND-SAUSAGE MINI PIZZAS

makes: 6 servings hands-on time: 20 min. total time: 40 min.

- 1 **lb. prepared pizza dough, at room temperature**
- 1 **lb. turkey sausage, casings removed**

Basic Tomato Sauce (page 8)

- 3 **cups (12 oz.) shredded Italian three-cheese blend**

Toppings: grated Parmesan cheese, sliced fresh mozzarella, turkey pepperoni, dried Italian seasoning, small basil leaves

1. Preheat oven to 400°. Divide dough in half. Roll each half into an 8-inch circle. Place dough rounds on 2 lightly greased baking sheets. Bake at 400° for 7 minutes.

2. Cook sausage in a large nonstick skillet over medium-high heat 9 to 11 minutes or until meat crumbles and is no longer pink; drain.

3. Spread about ⅓ cup Basic Tomato Sauce evenly over each pizza crust; top each pizza with ½ cup cheese, ⅓ cup cooked sausage, and desired toppings.

4. Bake at 400° for 8 to 10 minutes or until crust is golden and cheese is melted.

serve with
FRESH FRUIT SALAD WITH YOGURT

makes: 8 servings
hands-on time: 10 min.
total time: 10 min.

- 4 **cups fresh pineapple chunks**
- 1 **qt. strawberries, sliced in half**
- 3 **cups seedless green grapes**
- 2 **mangoes, peeled and sliced**
- 2 **(4-oz.) containers fresh raspberries**
- 2 **cups Greek yogurt**
- 1 **Tbsp. dark brown sugar**
- 1 **Tbsp. honey**

1. Toss together first 5 ingredients in a large serving bowl. Spoon yogurt into a separate serving bowl; sprinkle yogurt with sugar, and drizzle with honey. Serve fruit with yogurt mixture.

TURKEY SAUSAGE CALZONES

makes: 4 servings   hands-on time: 20 min.   total time: 45 min.

2   (4-oz.) links mild Italian turkey sausage, casings removed

2   tsp. vegetable oil

⅓   cup chopped red bell pepper

¾   cup sliced fresh mushrooms

3   Tbsp. chopped pimiento-stuffed green olives

⅛   tsp. dried oregano leaves

⅛   tsp. dried basil leaves

⅛   tsp. dried crushed red pepper

1   (13.8-oz.) can refrigerated classic pizza crust

⅓   cup pizza sauce

1   cup (4 oz.) shredded mozzarella cheese

1   large egg, slightly beaten

Additional pizza sauce, heated, if desired

PIZZA POINTER

For best results, dip fork in flour before crimping edges of each filled calzone.

1. Preheat oven to 400°. Lightly spray baking sheet with cooking spray. In 10-inch skillet, cook sausage over medium-high heat 6 minutes, stirring frequently, until sausage crumbles and is no longer pink. Remove sausage to bowl. In same skillet, heat oil over medium-high heat. Cook bell pepper and mushrooms in oil 5 minutes, stirring frequently, until tender. Add vegetables to sausage. Stir in olives, oregano, basil, and red pepper flakes.

2. Unroll dough on baking sheet. Starting at center, press dough into a 14- x 10-inch rectangle; cut into 4 (7- x 5-inch) rectangles. Spoon 1 slightly heaping Tbsp. pizza sauce onto each rectangle to within ½ inch of edge. Top half of each rectangle with sausage mixture and cheese, spreading to within ½ inch of edge. Fold dough in half over filling; press edges firmly with a fork to seal. Brush with egg.

3. Bake at 400° for 20 to 25 minutes or until golden brown. Serve warm calzones with warm pizza sauce for dipping, if desired.

FOUR-CHEESE PIZZA

makes: 5 servings hands-on time: 30 min. total time: 40 min.

Yellow cornmeal

1 lb. prepared pizza dough, at room temperature

1 Tbsp. olive oil

2 Tbsp. chopped garlic

⅓ cup (about 3 oz.) part-skim ricotta cheese

¼ cup (1 oz.) crumbled Gorgonzola cheese

1¼ oz. soft cow's milk cheese, such as Taleggio or Brie, thinly sliced

¼ cup (1 oz.) finely grated Parmigiano-Reggiano cheese

2 Tbsp. chopped fresh chives

PIZZA POINTER

Use whatever cheeses your family loves; mozzarella, fontina, Asiago, and feta are all great options.

1. Position oven rack in lowest setting. Place a pizza stone or heavy baking sheet on bottom rack in oven. Preheat oven to 550° (keep pizza stone or baking sheet in oven as it preheats). Preheat pizza stone or baking sheet 30 minutes before baking pizza.

2. Sprinkle cornmeal on a lightly floured baking sheet without raised edges. Press dough into a 12-inch circle on prepared pan. Crimp edges to form a ½-inch border.

3. Combine 1 Tbsp. oil and garlic; gently brush garlic mixture evenly over dough, leaving a ½-inch border. Spread ricotta evenly over dough; arrange Gorgonzola and Taleggio evenly over ricotta. Top with Parmigiano-Reggiano. Slide pizza onto preheated pizza stone or heavy baking sheet, using a spatula as a guide. Bake at 550° for 10 minutes or until crust is golden. Sprinkle with chives before serving.

BACON-AND-EGG BREAKFAST PIZZA

makes: 8 servings   hands-on time: 15 min.   total time: 40 min.

Bacon, cheese, and potatoes turn up the flavor on this kid-approved pizza. Reheat leftovers on a griddle or in a skillet over medium heat to get a crisp crust without overcooking the filling.

1   (8-oz.) can refrigerated crescent roll dough

vegetable cooking spray

1   cup frozen shredded or diced hash brown potatoes, thawed

6   center-cut bacon slices, cooked and crumbled

1   cup (4 oz.) reduced-fat shredded extra sharp Cheddar cheese

8   large egg whites, lightly beaten

¼   tsp. salt

⅛   tsp. freshly ground pepper

2   Tbsp. freshly grated Parmesan cheese

1. Preheat oven to 375°.

2. Unroll dough, and separate into triangles. Press triangles together to form a single 10-inch round crust on a 12-inch pizza pan coated with cooking spray. Crimp edges of dough with fingers to form a rim.

3. Top prepared dough with potatoes, bacon, and Cheddar cheese. Carefully pour egg whites over cheese; sprinkle with salt, pepper, and Parmesan cheese.

4. Bake at 375° for 23 minutes or until crust is browned.

serve with
BLACKBERRY SMOOTHIES

makes: 4 servings
hands-on time: 5 min.
total time: 5 min.

1   cup fat-free milk

1   pt. vanilla low-fat frozen yogurt, softened

1   medium banana, coarsely chopped

½   cup fresh blackberries

1. Process all ingredients in a blender until smooth, stopping to scrape down sides. Serve immediately.

BREAKFAST FOR DINNER!

GARDEN
FRESH

TOMATO-AND-CORN PIZZA

makes: 4 servings   hands-on time: 10 min.   total time: 44 min.

2   small plum tomatoes, sliced

¼   tsp. salt

⅛   tsp. freshly ground pepper

1   (14-oz.) Italian pizza crust

Parchment paper

⅓   cup refrigerated light pesto sauce

½   cup fresh corn kernels

¼   cup grated Parmesan cheese

1   tsp. sugar

8   oz. fresh mozzarella cheese, sliced

3   Tbsp. fresh whole or torn basil leaves

1. Preheat oven to 450°. Place tomato slices on paper towels. Sprinkle with salt and pepper; let stand 20 minutes.

2. Place pizza crust on a parchment paper-lined baking sheet; spread with pesto. Stir together corn, Parmesan, and sugar. Top pizza with corn mixture, tomatoes, and mozzarella slices.

3. Bake at 450° for 14 minutes or until cheese is melted and golden. Remove from oven, and top with basil leaves.

Substitute thawed, frozen whole kernel corn so you can skip the step of cutting it off the cob.

SPEED IT UP!

CHICKEN ALFREDO PIZZA

makes: 6 servings   hands-on time: 20 min.   total time: 30 min.

Chicken Alfredo transforms from a classic pasta to yummy pizza in this recipe.

Vegetable cooking spray

1   lb. prepared pizza dough, at room temperature

All-purpose flour

Yellow cornmeal

¾   cup Easy Alfredo Sauce (page 11)

1   (6-oz.) package fresh baby spinach

2   cups chopped cooked chicken

1½   cups (6 oz.) shredded fontina cheese

2   tsp. lemon juice

¼   tsp. salt

¼   tsp. pepper

1. Coat a cold cooking grate of grill with cooking spray, and place on grill. Preheat grill to 300° to 350° (medium) heat.

2. Divide dough into 6 equal portions. Lightly sprinkle flour on a large surface. Roll each portion into a 6-inch round (about ¼ inch thick). Carefully transfer pizza dough rounds to a cutting board or baking sheet sprinkled with cornmeal.

3. Slide pizza dough rounds onto cooking grate of grill; spread Easy Alfredo Sauce over rounds; top with spinach, chicken, and cheese. Sprinkle with lemon juice, salt, and pepper.

4. Grill, covered with grill lid, 4 minutes. Rotate pizzas one-quarter turn, and grill, covered with grill lid, 5 to 6 more minutes or until pizza crusts are cooked. Serve immediately.

PIZZA POINTER

Be sure to lightly grease the grill grates before lighting the grill. If you wait until after it's heated, the oil could flare up.

CHICKEN PARMESAN PIZZA

makes: 4 servings hands-on time: 14 min. total time: 30 min.

1 (10-oz.) package frozen garlic bread loaf

½ cup canned pizza sauce

6 deli fried chicken strips

1 cup (4 oz.) shredded Italian three-cheese blend

2 Tbsp. chopped fresh basil

1. Preheat oven to 400°. Arrange garlic bread, buttered sides up, on a baking sheet.

2. Bake at 400° for 8 to 9 minutes or until bread is lightly browned. Spread pizza sauce over garlic bread.

3. Cut chicken strips into ½-inch pieces, and arrange over pizza sauce. Sprinkle with cheese and basil.

4. Bake at 400° for 8 to 10 minutes or until cheese melts. Serve immediately.

serve with

EASY CAESAR SALAD

makes: 4 servings
hands-on time: 5 min.
total time: 5 min.

1 head romaine lettuce, torn

Freshly cracked pepper

Grated Parmesan cheese

Caesar dressing

Croutons

1. Toss together first 3 ingredients and top with Caesar dressing and croutons.

BUFFALO CHICKEN PIZZA

makes: 4 servings   hands-on time: 6 min.   total time: 16 min.

If you love Buffalo wings and pizza, this fun flavor combo over a grilled crust is sure to please.

Vegetable cooking spray

½   cup Buffalo-style hot sauce

1   (14-oz.) Italian pizza crust

2   cups chopped rotisserie chicken

1   cup (4 oz.) shredded provolone cheese

¼   cup crumbled blue cheese

1   Tbsp. chopped green onions

1. Coat cold cooking grate of grill with cooking spray, and place on grill. Preheat grill to 300° to 350° (medium) heat.

2. Spread hot sauce over crust, and layer with next 3 ingredients.

3. Place crust directly on cooking grate. Grill, covered with grill lid, 4 minutes. Rotate pizza one-quarter turn, and grill, covered with grill lid, 5 to 6 more minutes or until thoroughly heated. Sprinkle with green onions, and serve immediately.

Pizza Pointer

To make an oven-baked pizza instead, assemble pizza as directed, and bake according to package directions for pizza crust.

CHICKEN-AND-HERB WHITE PIZZA

makes: 6 servings   hands-on time: 20 min.   total time: 52 min.

Béchamel is often used in lasagna or in mac-and-cheese. Here, it's flavored with garlic and cheese, and replaces tomato sauce to make a delicious pizza.

1   Tbsp. butter

2   garlic cloves, minced

2   Tbsp. all-purpose flour

½   tsp. freshly ground pepper

¾   cup 2% reduced-fat milk

½   cup (2 oz.) freshly grated pecorino Romano cheese

Yellow cornmeal

1   lb. prepared pizza dough, at room temperature

1½   cups shredded boneless, skinless rotisserie chicken breast

¼   cup diced red onion

1   Tbsp. chopped fresh oregano

1   Tbsp. chopped fresh chives

1   Tbsp. chopped fresh parsley

1. Position oven rack in lowest setting. Preheat oven to 450°.

2. Melt butter in a medium saucepan over medium heat. Add garlic; cook 30 seconds, stirring constantly. Add flour and pepper; cook 1 minute, stirring constantly with a whisk. Gradually add milk, stirring constantly with a whisk. Cook 3 minutes or until thickened and bubbly, stirring constantly with a whisk. Remove from heat; add cheese, stirring until cheese melts.

3. Sprinkle a baking sheet with cornmeal; roll dough into a 12-inch circle on prepared baking sheet. Spread cheese mixture over dough, leaving a ½-inch border. Top with chicken and onion. Bake at 450° on bottom rack in oven 17 minutes or until crust is golden. Sprinkle with herbs. Cut pizza into 6 wedges.

PEPPERONI DEEP-DISH PIZZA

makes: 6 servings hands-on time: 10 min. total time: 35 min.

A bready crust, plenty of cheese, and America's favorite pizza topping: This pie satisfies several cravings at once.

1½ **lb. prepared pizza dough, at room temperature**

Vegetable cooking spray

1¼ **cups (5 oz.) shredded part-skim mozzarella cheese, divided**

1½ **cups Basic Pizza Sauce (page 9)**

2 **oz. pepperoni slices**

2 **Tbsp. freshly grated Parmigiano-Reggiano cheese**

Use 1½ cups jarred pizza sauce to make this classic pizza super-fast.

Speed It Up!

1. Roll dough into a 14- x 11-inch rectangle on a lightly floured surface. Press dough into bottom and partially up sides of a 13- x 9-inch metal baking pan coated with cooking spray. Cover dough loosely with plastic wrap.

2. Position oven rack in lowest setting; place a baking sheet on the rack. Preheat oven to 450° (keep baking sheet in oven as it preheats).

3. Remove plastic wrap from dough. Arrange ¾ cup mozzarella evenly over dough; top with Basic Pizza Sauce, pepperoni, Parmigiano-Reggiano, and remaining ½ cup mozzarella. Place pan on baking sheet in oven; bake at 450° for 25 minutes or until crust is golden. Cut pizza into 6 rectangles.

PIZZA BREAD ROLLUPS

makes: 4 to 6 servings hands-on time: 6 min. total time: 16 min.

This recipe is a great lunchbox treat, an after-school go-to, or an easy dinner.

- 1 **(3.5-oz.) package sliced turkey pepperoni**
- 1 **(13.8-oz.) can refrigerated pizza crust dough**
- 1 **large egg, lightly beaten and divided**
- 1 **cup (4 oz.) shredded sharp Cheddar cheese**
- 1 **tsp. dried Italian seasoning**
- **Pasta sauce (optional)**

PIZZA POINTER

Cooking the pepperoni between layers of paper towels helps avoid a greasy mess.

1. Preheat oven to 375°. Cook pepperoni slices between layers of paper towels in microwave at HIGH for 1 minute.

2. Unroll dough onto a jelly-roll pan to ¼-inch thickness. Brush lightly with egg. Sprinkle with cheese and pepperoni. Roll up, jelly-roll fashion.

3. Place dough on a lightly greased baking sheet. Curl dough into a circle, pinching edges together to seal. Brush with egg, and sprinkle with dried Italian seasoning.

4. Bake at 375° for 30 to 35 minutes or until golden. Cut into 2-inch-thick slices. Serve with with warm pasta sauce, if desired.

MACARONI PIZZA

makes: 1 (12-inch) pizza hands-on time: 15 min. total time: 50 min.

Macaroni in a pizza? Super-cheesy pasta plus pepperoni is super fun!

8 oz. hot cooked elbow macaroni

4 (1-oz.) processed American cheese slices, cut into thin strips

2 large eggs, lightly beaten

1 tsp. peanut oil

1 (7-oz.) jar pizza sauce

2 cups (8 oz.) shredded mozzarella cheese

1½ oz. sliced pepperoni

1. Preheat oven to 350°. Stir together hot macaroni and American cheese in a large bowl until cheese melts. Cool. Stir in eggs.

2. Brush peanut oil on a 12-inch pizza pan with sides. Spread macaroni mixture evenly in pan.

3. Bake at 350° for 10 minutes. Spread with sauce; top with mozzarella cheese and pepperoni. Bake 15 more minutes or until cheese melts.

serve with

BANANA-BERRY FREEZER POPS

makes: 10 pops
hands-on time: 15 min.
total time: 4 hours, 15 min.

3 cups fresh or frozen berries

½ cup honey

1 cup low-fat vanilla yogurt

1 banana

10 (2-oz.) pop molds

Craft sticks

1. Bring berries and honey to a boil. Reduce heat; simmer 5 minutes. Pour mixture through a wire-mesh strainer into a bowl, using back of a spoon to squeeze out juice and pulp. Discard solids. Cover and chill 30 minutes.

2. Process yogurt and banana in a blender; pour into pop molds, alternating with berry mixture. Top with lid, and insert craft sticks. Freeze for 4 hours.

Note: If you don't have frozen pop molds, you can use 2-oz. paper or plastic cups.

ULTIMATE CHEESEBURGER PIZZA

makes: 4 servings hands-on time: 15 min. total time: 29 min.

1   (14.5-oz.) can whole tomatoes, drained and chopped

1   tsp. bottled minced garlic

1   (12-inch) prebaked pizza crust

1½   cups (6 oz.) shredded Cheddar cheese

1½   cups cooked and crumbled ground beef (about ½ lb.)

¼   cup chopped green onions

½   tsp. salt

1. Preheat oven to 450°. Stir together tomatoes and garlic. Spread crust evenly with tomato mixture, and sprinkle with cheese, ground beef, green onions, and salt.

2. Bake at 450° for 12 to 14 minutes or until cheese is melted.

Pizza Pointer

To avoid having to get out the cutting board, you can crush whole tomatoes with clean hands instead of chopping them, or snip them into pieces with kitchen shears.

serve with

SALT & PEPPER OVEN FRIES

makes: 8 to 10 servings
hands-on time: 5 min.
total time: 35 min.

1   (26-oz.) package frozen extra-crispy French fried potatoes

¾   tsp. freshly ground pepper

½   tsp. kosher salt

1. Preheat oven to 425°. Arrange potatoes in a single layer on 2 lightly greased 15- x 10-inch jelly-roll pans. Bake 15 minutes, placing 1 pan on middle oven rack and other pan on lower oven rack. Switch pans, and bake 12 to 15 more minutes or until lightly browned. Sprinkle with pepper and salt, tossing lightly. Serve immediately.

Note: We tested with Ore-Ida Extra Crispy Fast Food Fries.

TACO PIZZAS

makes: 6 to 8 servings hands-on time: 25 min. total time: 40 min.

1 lb. ground pork*

1 (1.25-oz.) envelope 40%-less-sodium taco seasoning mix

¼ cup chopped fresh cilantro

1 (11-oz.) can Mexican-style corn, drained and rinsed

1 (10-oz.) can mild diced tomatoes and green chiles, drained

1½ cups (6 oz.) shredded colby-Jack cheese blend

1 (24-oz.) package prebaked pizza crusts

1 (16-oz.) can fat-free refried beans

Toppings: shredded lettuce, sour cream

Garnish: cilantro sprig

Pizza Pointer

This recipe makes 2 (12-inch) pizzas. If your family doesn't eat both pizzas on the same night, save half the ingredients for the second pizza for another meal.

1. Preheat oven to 425°. Cook pork in a large skillet over medium-high heat 5 minutes, stirring until meat crumbles and is no longer pink; drain well on paper towels. Wipe out skillet with a paper towel. Return pork to skillet; stir in taco seasoning mix and ⅔ cup water; cook according to package directions on seasoning mix. Remove mixture from heat, and stir in chopped cilantro and next 3 ingredients.

2. Place pizza crusts on baking sheets. Spread beans over crusts, leaving a ¼-inch border around edges. Top beans with pork mixture.

3. Bake, 1 pizza at a time, at 425° for 6 to 8 minutes or until thoroughly heated and cheese melts. Remove from oven, and let stand 5 minutes. Repeat with remaining pizza. Serve with desired toppings. Garnish, if desired.

* 1 lb. ground chuck may be substituted for ground pork.

Note: We tested with Old El Paso 40% Less Sodium Taco Seasoning Mix and Mama Mary's Traditional Gourmet Pizza Crusts (2 per package).

TACOS BY THE SLICE!

ITALIAN SAUSAGE BREAD PIZZA

makes: 8 servings hands-on time: 25 min. total time: 35 min.

1 lb. ground mild or spicy Italian pork sausage

2 Tbsp. olive oil

1 onion, halved, thinly sliced

2 garlic cloves, finely chopped

1 cup pizza sauce or tomato pasta sauce

1½ tsp. dried oregano leaves

¼ tsp. dried crushed red pepper

¼ tsp. salt

1 loaf French bread (about 14 inches long)

⅔ cup ricotta cheese

2 cups (8 oz.) shredded mozzarella cheese

¼ cup grated Parmesan cheese

Garnish: chopped fresh parsley

1. Preheat oven to 425°. Lightly spray a large baking sheet with cooking spray.

2. In a 12-inch skillet, cook sausage over medium-high heat 8 minutes, stirring occasionally, until sausage crumbles and is no longer pink. Push sausage to edges of skillet; add 1 Tbsp. oil. Add onion and garlic; cook 5 minutes, stirring occasionally, until onion is softened. Remove from heat; stir in pizza sauce, oregano, red pepper, and salt.

3. With serrated knife, cut bread in half lengthwise; scoop out center of each bread half, leaving ½-inch border (discard removed bread or reserve for making breadcrumbs). Place bread halves on prepared baking sheet. Spread one-third cup ricotta cheese down center of each; top evenly with sausage mixture, mozzarella cheese, and Parmesan cheese. Drizzle loaves with remaining 1 Tbsp. oil.

4. Bake at 425° for 6 minutes or until thoroughly heated and cheese is melted. Sprinkle with chopped fresh parsley, if desired.

CROWD FAVORITE!

BARBECUE PORK PIZZA

makes: 6 servings   hands-on time: 15 min.   total time: 35 min.

Vegetable cooking spray

1   Tbsp. olive oil

1   medium-size red onion, halved lengthwise, sliced

1   (11-oz.) can refrigerated thin pizza crust

¾   cup barbecue sauce

2   cups shredded barbecue pork (¾ lb.)

1½ cups (6 oz.) shredded Monterey Jack cheese

1   cup (4 oz.) shredded mozzarella cheese

Garnishes: chopped fresh cilantro, chopped green onions

1. Preheat oven to 425°. Coat a 15- x 10-inch or larger baking sheet with cooking spray.

2. In a 10-inch skillet, heat oil over medium heat. Cook red onion in oil 5 to 8 minutes, stirring occasionally, until tender. Remove from heat; set aside.

3. Unroll dough on prepared baking sheet; starting at center, press out dough into a 15- x 10-inch rectangle. Spread barbecue sauce evenly over dough. Top with red onion, pork, and cheeses.

4. Bake at 425° for 15 to 16 minutes or until crust is golden brown and cheese is melted.

PIZZA POINTER

Purchase pulled pork from your favorite barbecue restaurant, and use the restaurant's barbecue sauce as the base for this pizza.

serve with

TROPICAL SHAKE

makes: 4 servings
hands-on time: 8 min.
total time: 1 hour, 38 min.

1   medium-size ripe banana, cut into 1-inch slices

2   tsp. lemon juice

1   medium mango, peeled and cut into pieces

1½ cups pineapple-orange juice, chilled

1   (8-oz.) container fat-free vanilla yogurt

1. Toss banana with lemon juice; drain, reserving lemon juice. Place banana slices on a baking sheet, and freeze 1 hour and 30 minutes.

2. Process frozen banana slices, reserved lemon juice, mango, 1½ cups pineapple-orange juice, and yogurt in a blender until smooth, stopping to scrape down sides. Pour into chilled glasses; serve immediately.

CHOCOLATE-PEANUT BUTTER PIZZA

makes: 16 servings hands-on time: 5 min. total time: 45 min.

1   (18-oz.) roll refrigerated sugar cookie dough

½   cup creamy peanut butter

1¼ cups milk chocolate and peanut butter morsels

¼   cup miniature candy-coated chocolate pieces

¼   cup chopped salted peanuts

Hot Fudge Sauce

1. Preheat oven to 350°. Spread dough evenly on bottom and up sides of a lightly greased 12-inch pizza pan.

2. Bake at 350° on bottom rack for 20 to 25 minutes or until golden brown. Remove from oven, and cool 15 minutes.

3. Spread peanut butter evenly on top of cookie. Sprinkle with morsels, chocolate pieces, and peanuts. Cut into 16 wedges. Drizzle with Hot Fudge Sauce.

HOT FUDGE SAUCE

makes: about 1 cup
hands-on time: 5 min.
total time: 5 min.

1   (4-oz.) semisweet chocolate baking bar, chopped

¾   cup heavy cream

1. Microwave chocolate and cream in a small microwave-safe bowl at HIGH 1½ minutes or until chocolate melts and mixture is smooth, stirring at 30-second intervals.

Pizza Pointer

Dust your fingertips with powdered sugar to spread the cookie dough without sticking.

METRIC EQUIVALENTS

The information in the following charts is provided to help cooks outside the United States successfully use the recipes in this book. All equivalents are approximate.

Equivalents for Different Types of Ingredients

Standard Cup	Fine Powder (ex. flour)	Grain (ex. rice)	Granular (ex. sugar)	Liquid Solids (ex. butter)	Liquid (ex. milk)
1	140 g	150 g	190 g	200 g	240 ml
¾	105 g	113 g	143 g	150 g	180 ml
⅔	93 g	100 g	125 g	133 g	160 ml
½	70 g	75 g	95 g	100 g	120 ml
⅓	47 g	50 g	63 g	67 g	80 ml
¼	35 g	38 g	48 g	50 g	60 ml
⅛	18 g	19 g	24 g	25 g	30 ml

Liquid Ingredients by Volume

¼ tsp	=			1 ml
½ tsp	=			2 ml
1 tsp	=			5 ml
3 tsp	=	1 Tbsp =	½ fl oz =	15 ml
2 Tbsp	=	⅛ cup =	1 fl oz =	30 ml
4 Tbsp	=	¼ cup =	2 fl oz =	60 ml
5⅓ Tbsp	=	⅓ cup =	3 fl oz =	80 ml
8 Tbsp	=	½ cup =	4 fl oz =	120 ml
10⅔ Tbsp	=	⅔ cup =	5 fl oz =	160 ml
12 Tbsp	=	¾ cup =	6 fl oz =	180 ml
16 Tbsp	=	1 cup =	8 fl oz =	240 ml
1 pt	=	2 cups =	16 fl oz =	480 ml
1 qt	=	4 cups =	32 fl oz =	960 ml
			33 fl oz =	1000 ml = 1 l

Dry Ingredients by Weight

(To convert ounces to grams, multiply the number of ounces by 30.)

1 oz	=	¹⁄₁₆ lb	=	30 g
4 oz	=	¼ lb	=	120 g
8 oz	=	½ lb	=	240 g
12 oz	=	¾ lb	=	360 g
16 oz	=	1 lb	=	480 g

Length

(To convert inches to centimeters, multiply the number of inches by 2.5.)

1 in =			2.5 cm
6 in =	½ ft	=	15 cm
12 in =	1 ft	=	30 cm
36 in =	3 ft = 1 yd	=	90 cm
40 in		=	100 cm = 1 m

Cooking/Oven Temperatures

	Fahrenheit	Celsius	Gas Mark
Freeze Water	32° F	0° C	
Room Temp.	68° F	20° C	
Boil Water	212° F	100° C	
Bake	325° F	160° C	3
	350° F	180° C	4
	375° F	190° C	5
	400° F	200° C	6
	425° F	220° C	7
	450° F	230° C	8
Broil			Grill

INDEX

A

Accompaniments. *See also* **Beverages; Salads**
Black Beans, Zippy, 64
Bread, Garlic-Herb, 117
Broccoli, Roasted, 76
Carrots, Honeyed, 157
Freezer Pops, Banana-Berry, 207
Fries, Salt & Pepper Oven, 209
Green Beans, Nutty, 128
Rolls, Easy Garlic, 67
Spinach-and-Red-Pepper Sauté, 52
Vegetables, Roasted, 113
Zucchini and Bell Pepper, Sautéed, 98
Zucchini Spears, Sautéed, 132
Apple–Goat Cheese Pizza, 138
Apple-Pineapple Dessert Pizza, 177
Artichoke Pizza with Arugula & Prosciutto, 151
Artichokes, Greek Pizza with Chicken &, 161
Arugula
Pizza
Artichoke Pizza with Arugula & Prosciutto, 151
Bacon, Tomato & Arugula Pizza, 157
The Farmer's Pizza, 158
Grilled Pizza with Steak, Pear & Arugula, 171
Oven-Baked Pizza with Steak, Pear & Arugula, 171
Salad, Arugula–Grape Tomato, 53
Asparagus & Basil Pizza, Tomato, 43
Asparagus and Caramelized Onion, Grilled Pizza with, 143

B

Bacon
Bacon, Onion & Mushroom Pizza, 92
Bacon, Tomato & Arugula Pizza, 157
Bacon-and-Egg Breakfast Pizza, 192
Beef & Bacon Pizza, 91
Carne Lover's Pizza, 97
Turkey Club Pizza, 164
Balsamic Dressing, Spinach Salad with, 51
Balsamic Vegetable Pita Pizzas, 36
Balsamic Vegetables, 36
Basil
Pesto, Basil, 12
Pesto, Basil-Mint, 146
Pizza
Goat Cheese, Tomato & Basil Pizza, 40
Mozzarella & Basil Mini Pizza, 73
Pizza Margherita, 70
Tomato, Asparagus & Basil Pizza, 43
Beans. *See also* **Green Beans**
Black Beans
Black Bean Salsa, 162

Santa Fe Pizza, 60
Southwestern Pizza, 162
Zippy Black Beans, 64
Taco Pizzas, 210
Beef
Calzones, Beef, 109
Calzones, Spinach & Beef, 110
Pizza
Beef & Bacon Pizza, 91
Beef & Pepperoni Pizza, 89
Grilled Pizza with Steak, Pear & Arugula, 171
Oven-Baked Pizza with Steak, Pear & Arugula, 171
Ultimate Cheeseburger Pizza, 209
Beet Pizza, Roasted, 125
Beverages
Shake, Hot Fudge Sundae, 183
Shake, Tropical, 215
Smoothies, Blackberry, 192
Blackberry Smoothies, 192
Breakfast Pizzas
Bacon-and-Egg Breakfast Pizza, 192
Sunny-Side-Up Pizza, 46
Broccoli, Roasted, 76
Broccoli-Cheese Calzones, 109

C

Calzones
Beef Calzones, 109
Broccoli-Cheese Calzones, 109
Chicken Alfredo Calzones, 110
Muffuletta Calzones, 167
Pepperoni Calzones, Cheesy, 113
Spinach & Beef Calzones, 110

Turkey Sausage Calzones, 189
Carrot-Cucumber Slaw, 59
Carrots, Honeyed, 157
Cheese Pizza, Four-, 190
Cheese Pizza, Ultimate, 76
Chicken
    Calzones, Chicken Alfredo, 110
    Pizza
        Barbecue Chicken Pizza, 57
        Bistro Grilled Chicken
            Pizza, 54
        Buffalo Chicken Pizza, 201
        Chicago Deep-Dish Pizza, 102
        Chicken Alfredo Pizza, 196
        Chicken-and-Herb White
            Pizza, 202
        Chicken Fajita Pizza, 53
        Chicken Parmesan Pizza, 199
        Greek Pizza with Chicken &
            Artichokes, 161
        Peach & Gorgonzola Chicken
            Pizza, 51
        Southwestern Pizza, 162
Chocolate
    Pizza, Chocolate–Peanut
        Butter, 217
    Pizza Dolce, 176
    Sauce, Hot Fudge, 217
    Shake, Hot Fudge Sundae, 183
Corn
    Mexican Pizza, 64
    Taco Pizzas, 210
    Tomato-and-Corn Pizza, 195
Cucumber Slaw, Carrot-, 59
Cucumbers, Sesame-Ginger, 143

D

Dates, Prosciutto & Almonds,
    Gorgonzola Pizza with, 155
Deep-Dish Pizzas
    Chicago Deep-Dish Pizza, 102

Italian Sausage Deep-Dish
    Pizza, 98
Pepperoni Deep-Dish
    Pizza, 204
Dessert Pizzas
    Apple-Pineapple Dessert
        Pizza, 177
    Chocolate–Peanut Butter
        Pizza, 217
    Pizza Dolce, 176
Divided Pizza
    Have-It-Your-Way Pizza, 80
Dough. *See Pizza* **Dough**

E

Eggplant Pizza, Garden, 39
Eggs
    Bacon-and-Egg Breakfast
        Pizza, 192
    Mini Pesto Pizzas with Zucchini
        Ribbons, Fontina &
        Eggs, 146
    Sunny-Side-Up Pizza, 46

F

Fennel, in Sausage Pizza, 95
Figs, in Apple–Goat Cheese
    Pizza, 138
Flatbread Pizzas
    Balsamic Vegetable Pita
        Pizzas, 36
    Caramelized Onion
        Flatbread, 114
    Grape, Blue Cheese & Walnut
        Pizza, 141
    Mushroom Pizza Sticks, 24
    Pita Pizzas with Spinach,
        Fontina & Onions, 30
    Provençal Flatbread, 172
    Southwestern Pizza, 162

White Pizzas with Vegetables,
    Mini, 27
Focaccia, Cornbread, 175
Focaccia, Fresh Lemon Greens
    on Red Pepper, 118
Fruit. *See also* **specific fruits**
    Freezer Pops, Banana-
        Berry, 207
    Salad with Yogurt, Fresh
        Fruit, 186
    Shake, Tropical, 215

G

Garlic
    Bread, Garlic-Herb, 117
    Dressing, Mixed Greens with
        Garlic Oil, 70
    Pizza, Garlic–Mashed
        Potato, 34
    Pizza, Roasted Garlic, 144
    Rolls, Easy Garlic, 67
Grape, Blue Cheese & Walnut
    Pizza, 141
Grapefruit Salad, 104
Green Beans, Nutty, 128
Greens. *See* **Arugula; Spinach**
Grilled Pizzas
    Asparagus and Caramelized
        Onion, Grilled Pizza
        with, 143
    Chicken
        Bistro Grilled Chicken
            Pizza, 54
        Buffalo Chicken Pizza, 201
        Chicken Alfredo Pizza, 196
        Pear, Hazelnut & Gouda
            Pizzas, 134
        Shrimp-Pesto Pizzas, 149
        Steak, Pear & Arugula, Grilled
            Pizza with, 171

Tomato-Peach Pizza, Grilled, 128
Tomato Pizza, Grilled Heirloom, 45

H

Ham. *See also* **Prosciutto**
Antipasto Pizza, 104
Hawaiian Pizza, 59
Muffuletta Calzones, 167
Herbs. *See also* **Basil**
Bread, Garlic-Herb, 117
Coleslaw, Onion-and-Herb, 168
Pizza, Chicken-and-Herb White, 202
Provençal Flatbread, 172
Tart, Herbed Tomato, 126

M

"Meaty" Filling, 106
Mini Pizzas
Balsamic Vegetable Pita Pizzas, 36
Cheese-and-Sausage Mini Pizzas, 186
Mozzarella & Basil Mini Pizza, 73
Pesto Pizzas with Zucchini Ribbons, Fontina & Eggs, Mini, 146
Pita Pizzas with Spinach, Fontina & Onions, 30
White Pizzas with Vegetables, Mini, 27
Muffins, Pizza, 184
Mushrooms
Pizza
Bacon, Onion & Mushroom Pizza, 92
Caramelized Onion & Mushroom Pizza, 79

Portobello Pizza, 131
Roasted Mushroom & Shallot Pizza, 33
Pizza Sticks, Mushroom, 24
Roasted Mushrooms & Shallots, 33

N

Nuts
Chocolate–Peanut Butter Pizza, 217
Gorgonzola Pizza with Dates, Prosciutto & Almonds, 155
Grape, Blue Cheese & Walnut Pizza, 141
Pear, Hazelnut & Gouda Pizzas, 134

O

Olive Pizza, Pepperoni, Onion &, 84
Onions. *See also* **Shallots**
Coleslaw, Onion-and-Herb, 168
Flatbread, Caramelized Onion, 114
Pizza
Bacon, Onion & Mushroom Pizza, 92
Caramelized Onion & Mushroom Pizza, 79
Grilled Pizza with Asparagus and Caramelized Onion, 143
Pepperoni, Onion & Olive Pizza, 84
Pita Pizzas with Spinach, Fontina & Onions, 30
Sausage Pizza, 95
Orange Salad, Mandarin, 86

P

Pancetta, in The Farmer's Pizza, 158
Pasta
Pizza, Macaroni, 207
Salad, Bell Pepper Pasta, 80
Salad, Greek Pasta, 30
Peach & Gorgonzola Chicken Pizza, 51
Peach Pizza, Grilled Tomato–, 128
Pears
Grilled Pizza with Steak, Pear & Arugula, 171
Oven-Baked Pizza with Steak, Pear & Arugula, 171
Pear, Hazelnut & Gouda Pizzas, 134
Pepperoni
Calzones, Cheesy Pepperoni, 113
Muffins, Pizza, 184
Pizza
Beef & Pepperoni Pizza, 89
Carne Lover's Pizza, 97
Pepperoni, Onion & Olive Pizza, 84
Pepperoni Deep-Dish Pizza, 204
Pepperoni Pizza, 83
Whole Wheat Pepperoni Pizza, 86
Rolls, Stuffed Pizza, 183
Rollups, Pizza Bread, 206
Peppers
Focaccia, Fresh Lemon Greens on Red Pepper, 118
Pizza, Peppers-and-Cheese, 77
Pizza Supreme, 101
Salad, Bell Pepper Pasta, 80
Sauté, Spinach-and-Red-Pepper, 52

Sautéed Zucchini and Bell Pepper, 98

Pesto
Basil-Mint Pesto, 146
Basil Pesto, 12
Sun-Dried Tomato Pesto, 15

Pineapple
Apple-Pineapple Dessert Pizza, 177
Barbecued Pork & Pineapple Pizza, 168
Hawaiian Pizza, 59

Pizza Dough
Brick Oven Pizza Dough, 19
Easy Pizza Dough, 16
Gluten-Free Pizza Dough, 17
Sourdough Pizza Dough, 20–21
Whole Wheat Pizza Dough, 18

Pizza Sauce. *See Sauces*
Pops, Banana-Berry Freezer, 207

Pork. *See also* **Bacon; Ham; Pancetta; Prosciutto; Sausage**
Barbecue Pork Pizza, 215
Barbecued Pork & Pineapple Pizza, 168
Taco Pizzas, 210

Potatoes. *See also* **Sweet Potatoes**
Fries, Salt & Pepper Oven, 209
Pizza, Garlic–Mashed Potato, 34

Prosciutto
Artichoke Pizza with Arugula & Prosciutto, 151
Gorgonzola Pizza with Dates, Prosciutto & Almonds, 155
Prosciutto Pizza with Tangy White Sauce, 152

R

Rolls, Easy Garlic, 67
Rolls, Stuffed Pizza, 183
Rollups, Pizza Bread, 206

S

Salads
Arugula–Grape Tomato Salad, 53
Caesar Salad, Easy, 199
Coleslaw, Onion-and-Herb, 168
Cucumbers, Sesame-Ginger, 143
Fruit Salad with Yogurt, Fresh, 186
Grapefruit Salad, 104
Mandarin Orange Salad, 86
Mixed Greens with Dijon Vinaigrette, 43
Mixed Greens with Garlic Oil Dressing, 70
Pasta Salad, Bell Pepper, 80
Pasta Salad, Greek, 30
Romaine Salad, 83
Slaw, Carrot-Cucumber, 59
Spinach Salad with Balsamic Dressing, 51
Salsa, Black Bean, 162

Sauces. *See also* **Pesto**
Alfredo Sauce, Easy, 11
Hot Fudge Sauce, 217
Pizza Sauce, Basic, 9
Pizza Sauce, Spicy Tomato, 10
Tomato Sauce, Basic, 8
White Sauce, Prosciutto Pizza with Tangy, 152

Sausage. *See also* **Pepperoni**
Calzones, Muffuletta, 167
Calzones, Turkey Sausage, 189

Pizza
Antipasto Pizza, 104
Carne Lover's Pizza, 97
Cheese-and-Sausage Mini Pizzas, 186
Chicago Deep-Dish Pizza, 102
Italian Sausage Bread Pizza, 213
Italian Sausage Deep-Dish Pizza, 98
Mexican Pizza, 64
Pizza Supreme, 101
Santa Fe Pizza, 60
Sausage Pizza, 95
"The Works" Pizza, 99
Two-Tomato Turkey Sausage Pizza, 63
Shake, Hot Fudge Sundae, 183
Shake, Tropical, 215
Shallot Pizza, Roasted Mushroom &, 33
Shallots, Roasted Mushrooms &, 33

Shrimp
Pizza, Shrimp, 48
Pizzas, Shrimp-Pesto, 149
Poached Shrimp, Perfect, 48
Smoothies, Blackberry, 192
Sourdough Primary Batter, 21
Sourdough Starter, 21

Spinach
Calzones, Spinach & Beef, 110
Pita Pizzas with Spinach, Fontina & Onions, 30
Pizza, Sunny-Side-Up, 46
Salad with Balsamic Dressing, Spinach, 51
Sauté, Spinach-and-Red-Pepper, 52

Squares, Easy Pizza, 52
Sticks, Mushroom Pizza, 24
Sticks, Pizza, 180
Stromboli, Vegetarian, 106
Sweet Potato–Brie Pizza, 132
Sweet Potatoes, in Harvest
    Pizza, 137

T
Tart, Herbed Tomato, 126
Tomatoes
    Pesto, Sun-Dried Tomato, 15
    Pizza
        Bacon, Tomato & Arugula
            Pizza, 157
        Fresh Tomato–Feta Pizza, 74
        Goat Cheese, Tomato, & Basil
            Pizza, 40
        Grilled Heirloom Tomato
            Pizza, 45
        Grilled Tomato–Peach
            Pizza, 128
        Tomato, Asparagus & Basil
            Pizza, 43
        Tomato-and-Corn Pizza, 195

Two-Tomato Turkey Sausage
    Pizza, 63
Pizza Sauce, Basic, 9
Pizza Sauce, Spicy Tomato, 10
Roasted Zucchini &
    Tomatoes, 28
Salad, Arugula–Grape
    Tomato, 53
Sauce, Basic Tomato, 8
Tart, Herbed Tomato, 126
Topping, Tomato, 34
Turkey
Calzones, Turkey Sausage, 189
Pizza
    Harvest Pizza, 137
    Turkey Club Pizza, 164
    Two-Tomato Turkey Sausage
        Pizza, 63
Vegetables. *See also* **specific
    vegetables**
Balsamic Vegetables, 36
Calzones, Muffuletta, 167
Grilled Summer Veggies, 78
Pizza
    Antipasto Pizza, 104

Balsamic Vegetable Pita
    Pizzas, 36
Garden Eggplant Pizza, 39
Harvest Pizza, 137
Local Farmers' Market
    Pizza, 122
Mini White Pizzas with
    Vegetables, 27
Roasted Mushroom & Shallot
    Pizza, 33
Roasted Vegetable Pizza, 28
"The Works" Pizza, 99
Ultimate Veggie Pizza, 78
Roasted Vegetables, 113

Z
Zucchini
Mini Pesto Pizzas with Zucchini
    Ribbons, Fontina &
    Eggs, 146
Roasted Zucchini &
    Tomatoes, 28
Sautéed Zucchini and Bell
    Pepper, 98
Sautéed Zucchini Spears, 132

ISBN-13: 978-0-8487-3791-7
ISBN-10: 0-8487-3791-1
Library of Congress Control Number: 2013943043

Printed in the United States of America
First Printing 2013

Oxmoor House
Editorial Director: Leah McLaughlin
Creative Director: Felicity Keane
Brand Manager: Katie McHugh
Senior Editors: Heather Averett, Rebecca Brennan
Managing Editor: Rebecca Benton

Pizza Night!
Editor: Allison E. Cox
Art Director: Claire Cormany
Project Editor: Megan McSwain Yeatts
Assistant Designer: Allison Sperando Potter
Director, Test Kitchen: Elizabeth Tyler Austin
Recipe Developers and Testers: Wendy Ball, R.D.; Victoria E. Cox; Tamara Goldis; Stefanie Maloney; Callie Nash; Karen Rankin, Leah Van Deren
Recipe Editor: Alyson Moreland Haynes
Food Stylists: Margaret Monroe Dickey, Catherine Crowell Steele
Photography Director: Jim Bathie
Senior Photographer: Hélène Dujardin
Senior Photo Stylist: Kay E. Clarke
Photo Stylist: Mindi Shapiro Levine
Assistant Photo Stylist: Mary Louise Menendez
Senior Production Managers: Greg A. Amason, Susan Chodakiewicz

Contributors
Project Editor: Katie Strasser
Copy Editors: Donna Baldone, Barry Smith
Proofreader: Julie Bosche
Indexer: Mary Ann Laurens
Interns: Megan Branagh, Frances Gunnells, Susan Kemp, Sara Lyon, Staley McIlwain, Jeffrey Preis, Maria Sanders, Julia Sayers
Photographer: Johnny Autry
Photo Stylists: Charlotte Autry, Lydia Degaris Pursell
Food Stylists: Charlotte Autry, Marian Cooper Cairns

Time Home Entertainment Inc.
Publisher: Jim Childs
Vice President, Brand & Digital Strategy: Steven Sandonato
Executive Director, Marketing Services: Carol Pittard
Executive Director, Retail & Special Sales: Tom Mifsud
Director, Bookazine Development & Marketing: Laura Adam
Executive Publishing Director: Joy Butts
Associate Publishing Director: Megan Pearlman
Finance Director: Glenn Buonocore
Associate General Counsel: Helen Wan